Gender, Society & Development

Gender, citizenship and governance

A global source book

CRITICAL REVIEWS AND ANNOTATED

BIBLIOGRAPHIES SERIES

KIT (Royal Tropical Institute), The Netherlands

Oxfam GB

KIT (Royal Tropical Institute)
KIT Publishers
P.O. Box 95001
1090 HA AMSTERDAM
The Netherlands
Telephone: +31 (0) 20 568 8272
Telefax: +31 (0) 20 568 8286
E-mail: publishers@kit.nl
Website: www.kit.nl

Oxfam Publishing
274 Banbury Road
Oxford OX2 7DZ
United Kingdom
Telephone: +44 (0) 1865 311 311
Telefax: +44 (0) 1865 312 600
E-mail: publish@oxfam.org.uk
Website: www.oxfam.org.uk

Design: Grafisch Ontwerpbureau Agaatsz BNO,
Meppel
Cover: Ad van Helmond, Amsterdam
Printing: Meester & de Jonge, Lochem
ISBN 90 6832 724 0 (KIT Publishers edition)
available in the EC excluding UK and Ireland
ISBN 0 85598 528 3 (Oxfam GB edition)
available in the rest of the world
Printed and bound in The Netherlands

Gender, citizenship and governance.
A global source book
has been developed by KIT (Royal Tropical Institute)
in The Netherlands. It is co-published with Oxfam
GB to increase dissemination. KIT Publishers and
the authors are responsible for its content.

Oxfam GB is a registered charity no. 202918,
and is a member of Oxfam International

Other titles in the *Gender, Society & Development*
series:
• *Advancing women's status: women and men
  together?*
  M. de Bruyn (ed.)
• *Gender training. The source book.*
  S. Cummings, H. van Dam and M. Valk (eds.)
• *Women's information services and networks.
  A global source book.*
  S. Cummings, H. van Dam and M. Valk (eds.)
• *Institutionalizing gender equality. Commitment,
  policy and practice. A global source book.*
  H. van Dam, A. Khadar and M. Valk (eds.)
• *Gender perspectives on property and inheritance.
  A global source book*
  S. Cummings, H. van Dam, A. Khadar and M. Valk
  (eds.)
• *Natural resources management and gender.
  A global source book*
  H. van Dam, S. Cummings and M. Valk (eds.)

Gender, Society & Development

Gender, citizenship and governance
A global source book

Contents

Acknowledgements   7

Acronyms   9

Introduction: gender, citizenship and governance   13
Maitrayee Mukhopadhyay

Decentralization process and women: the case of Kerala, India   29
Aleyamma Vijayan

Engendering institutions in Pakistan   41
Naeem Mirza

Customary law reform in the new South Africa   51
Catherine Albertyn and Likhapha Mbatha

**A case study of the 50/50 campaign in Namibia, focusing on women's
grass-roots participation**   61
Liz Frank and Elizabeth Khaxas

Annotated bibliography   75
Guide to the bibliography   76
Annotated bibliography   77
Author index   125
Geographical index   127

Web resources   129

About the authors   133

Acknowledgements

A major objective of this publication was to document the experiences of various practitioners and experts in the South with respect to gender, citizenship and governance. The Editorial Team is delighted that it has been possible to realize this objective. We would like to record our warm and deep appreciation of the authors for their important contribution to this book.

Special thanks go to the Maitrayee Mukhopadhyay and her colleagues of KIT Gender for the stimulating role she played in the conception of this book. She has provided great support by sharing her experiences gained with the Gender, Citizenship and Governance programme. We would also like to thank Theresa Stanton for her contribution to the bibliography, as well as our colleagues in KIT Information and Library Services and KIT Publishers for their invaluable assistance.

Rinke, Sarah and Henk
Editorial Team, Gender, Society & Development

Acronyms

ADB	Asian Development Bank
AIDS	acquired immune deficiency syndrome
ANU	Australian National University
APWLD	Asia Pacific Forum on Women, Law and Development
BC	birth certificate
CAPWIP	Center for Asia Pacific Women in Politics
CALS	Centre for Applied Legal Studies, South Africa
CBO	community-based organization
CEDAW	Committee on the Elimination of Discrimination Against Women
CEDPA	Centre for Development and Population Activities
CLD	Center for Legislative Development
CoD	Congress of Democrats, Namibia
CSO	civil society organizations
DAC	Development Assistance Committee
DAW	United Nations Division for the Advancement of Women
DAWN	Development Alternatives with Women for a New Era
DDA	United Nations Department for Disarmament Affairs
DFAIT	Department of Foreign Affairs and International Trade, Canada
DFID	Department for International Development, United Kingdom
DTA	Democratic Turnhall Alliance, Namibia
ECDPM	European Centre for Development Policy Management, Netherlands
EU	European Union
FWCW	Fourth World Conference on Women
GBIs	gender budget initiatives
GCG	Gender, Citizenship and Governance programme, KIT (Royal Tropical Institute)
GETNET	Gender Education and Training Network, South Africa
GRB	gender-responsive budget
GRBI	Gender-Responsive Budget Initiative
GRC	Governance Resource Centre
GRGB	gender-responsive government budgeting
GTZ	German Technical Co-operation
HIPC	Heavily Indebted Poor Countries initiative
HIV	human immune deficiency virus
IA	International Alert
IAMWGE	Interagency Meeting on Women and Gender Equality
ICRC	International Committee of the Red Cross
ICRW	International Center for research on Women

ICTs	information and communication technologies
ID	identity card
IDEA	International Institute for Democracy and Electoral Assistance, Sweden
IDRC	International Development Research Centre, Canada
IDS	Institute of Development Studies, United Kingdom
IMF	International Monetary Fund
INSTRAW	International Research and Training Institute for the Advancement of Women
IPU	Inter-Parliamentary Union, Switzerland
IULA	International Union of Local Authorities, Netherlands
IWDC	International Women's Democracy Centre
KIT	Royal Tropical Institute/Koninklijk Instituut voor de Tropen)
LC	local council
LDF	Left Democratic Government, India
LGA	local government associations
LSGIs	Local self governing institutions
MDGs	Millennium Development Goals
MP	member of parliament
NCSW	National Commission on the Status of Women, Pakistan
NEPAD	New Partnership for African Development
NGDOs	non-governmental development organizations
NGOs	non-governmental organizations
NHGs	neighbourhood groups
NMW	national machinery for women
NRM	National Resistance Movement, Uganda
NUPI	Norwegian Institute of International Affairs
NWM	national women's machinery
NWMN	Namibian Women's Manifesto Network
OECD	Organization for Economic Co-operation and Development
PPC	People's planning campaign
PRA	participatory rural appraisal
PREM	Poverty Reduction and Economic Management, World Bank
PRIs	Panchayati Raj institutions
PRIO	International Peace Research Institute, Norway
PROWID	Promoting Women in Development grants programme
PRSP	Poverty Reduction Strategy Paper
RIRF-WLG	Regional Information Resource Facility-Women in Local Government
RWM	Rural Women's Movement, South Africa
SADC	Southern African Development Community
SALC	South African Law Commission
SAP	South Asia Partnership
SAPs	structural adjustment programmes
SHGs	self-help groups
SNV	Netherlands Development Organization
STIs	sexually transmitted infections
TA	technical assistance
TWN-Africa	Third World Network Africa

UDF	United Democratic Front, Namibia
UN	United Nations
UNDP	United Nations Development Programme
UNESCAP	United Nations Economic and Social Commission for Asia and the Pacific
UNHCR	United Nations High Commission for Refugees
UNICEF	United Nations International Children's Fund
UNIFEM	United Nations Development Fund for Women
UNRISD	United Nations Research Institute for Social Development, Switzerland
USAID	United States Agency for International Development
WBI	Women's Budget Initiative
WCP	Women's Component Plan
WEDO	Women's Environment and Development Organization
WiLDAF	Women in Law and Development in Africa
WILPF	Women's International League for Peace and Freedom
WISCOMP	Women in Security, Conflict Management and Peace, India
WLP	Women's Learning Partnership for Rights, Development, and Peace
WOUGNET	Women of Uganda Network
WP-GEN	Working Party on Gender Equality
ZWRCN	Zimbabwe Women's Resource Centre and Network

Maitrayee Mukhopadhyay

Introduction: gender, citizenship and governance

This volume brings together case studies of citizen action aimed at giving voice to women's needs and concerns, carving out spaces for equal participation of women and men in governance, and improving accountability and responsiveness of governance institutions to poor women's interests.

In 1999 KIT Gender, at the Royal Tropical Institute (KIT) in Amsterdam, initiated a three-year programme entitled 'Gender, Citizenship and Governance'. This programme aimed to contribute to the generation of knowledge and practice that would help to make gender equity and equality a core concern in the debate on and practice of good governance. It provided a framework to facilitate innovative gender and governance initiatives and was undertaken in collaboration with 16 organizations from India, Pakistan, Sri Lanka, Bangladesh, Namibia, Zambia, Zimbabwe and South Africa. The development of these partnerships and of collaborative action research was the cornerstone of the programme. The aim was to construct a forum for linking and learning, in the best traditions of participatory and action-oriented research, and contribute the insights generated to improving development policy and practice.

Why a programme on Gender, Citizenship and Governance?

In the 1990s the issue of good governance assumed enormous significance in the debates on global development. The concern with governance arose from the growing realization that conventional development efforts had failed to achieve desired ends, to eliminate poverty and inequality and to promote respect for human rights. The attention thus began to shift away from traditional development interventions towards a greater consideration for the way in which power was exercized in the management of economic and social resources for development.

The priorities of the good governance agenda differed according to the priorities and mandates of the donors and different actors involved in the debate. Despite differences in the priorities, the good governance agenda, by and large, envisaged building accountability of public administration institutions to the public they are supposed to serve. Typically this involved resourcing a wide variety of projects to improve the institutional capacity of various types of organizations and institutions, especially of governmental bodies. While some donors stressed democratic reforms, this mainly concentrated on the institutional design of the state involving reform of electoral systems, decentralization and devolution of government, and reform of administrative and legal systems.

introduction

Our concern was that the debates about and approaches to improving governance structures to obtain better development outcomes did not automatically address the question of gender inequality. If the desired outcome of good governance is distributional equity then gender equality should stand high on the agenda of this project. As for example, enhancing governmental capability to design, formulate and discharge its functions especially with regard to economic management does not necessarily entail recognizing the central contribution of unpaid labour (mostly performed by women) thereby excluding from public accountability a significant area of priorities and exacerbating the gender divide. Establishing the rule of law does not automatically translate into the legal recognition of violence against women as a crime. Expanding the scope of citizen participation in governance through decentralization of government does not by itself ensure that women and men will be represented on an equal basis. In all of these areas special efforts have been necessary to integrate gender equality concerns, which in turn has necessitated changes in institutional rules and practices.

It is with the above context in mind that the programme aimed to develop a range of good practices to bring about institutional change: changes in institutional rules and practices that would promote gender equality and enhance citizen participation. A related concern was that approaches to improving governance did not adequately recognize and resource the role of civil society institutions in creating the demand for democratic, accountable and just governance. Thus in order to build good practice on institutional change from a gender perspective the approach adopted was to resource civil society institutions.

Locating our work in the context of debates on citizenship and governance

What was the 'good governance' agenda?

In the 1990s the international financial institutions like the World Bank, bilateral donors and multilateral donors, such as the European Union and the Organization for Economic Cooperation and Development, highlighted the need for good governance to ensure that development aid had the desired results of bringing about economic, social and political changes in developing countries.

The priorities of the good governance agenda differed according to the priorities and mandates of the donors and different actors involved in the debate. For example, according to the Bretton Woods institutions (World Bank and International Monetary Fund) a good government is one that does not intervene in production, but limits itself to providing physical infrastructure, sound economic management, and builds a legal framework favourable to private property. On the other hand, some of the other multilateral and bilateral donors and donor groupings were more explicit about civil and political rights and democracy and therefore the need for political reform as part of the good governance agenda.

Despite differences in the priorities, the good governance agenda, by and large, envisaged building accountability of public administration institutions to the public they are supposed to serve. In terms of donor efforts to support 'good governance' in developing countries much of the resources went towards reforming the state and 'improving' public administration.

While promoting democratic structures in governance was suggested for achieving accountability, the formula for democratic reform concentrated more on the institutional design of the state involving reform of electoral systems, decentralization and devolution of government, reform of administrative and legal systems. In fact in much of development practice the term 'good governance' came to mean decentralization of government.

Enhancing popular participation was also recognized as a means for promoting better governance. Empowering groups, communities and organizations to negotiate with political institutions and bureaucracies was considered critical for influencing public policy, providing a check on government discretion, and enhancing the effectiveness and sustainability of development programmes. However, this approach received far less attention than the others mainly because while improving governance involved the exercise of power, which is a political exercise, international organizations and donors who sponsored the 'good governance' agenda could not be seen to become enmeshed in the internal politics of a country.

How globalization changed the context of governance

The 'good governance' agenda was by and large a donor-sponsored agenda occurring at a specific moment in international development. And this moment was and is what has come to be understood as the processes of globalization or global restructuring. The speed and range of the globalization of economics, politics, and culture occurring over the last two decades of the twentieth century but accelerated in the last decade, meant that there are more actors in governance than those we have traditionally associated with governance i.e. the state and civil society and political institutions. Governance of a people and society are today inextricably linked today with the policies and programmes of international development institutions, the international financial institutions as much as it is with the national or local governments, civil society and political institutions in a given country. As for example, recent feminist activism in some countries to provide a gender analysis of national budgets in order to highlight gender equity concerns in resource allocation comes at a time when most countries are subject to stringent macroeconomic reforms imposed by the international financial institutions. The latter do not necessarily allow for re-distributive measures that make the needs of human reproduction central, thereby marginalizing women's work. The implication is, therefore, that gender and development activists must learn to strategize at multiple levels of governance: national, regional and international.

According to Gita Sen (2002), globalization has broken three of the major social contracts that have existed in the world for at least fifty years. The first social contract that has broken down is that between workers and employers, framed as this relationship was in the right to collective bargaining and rights through social democracy. These have been significantly broken because of the extreme mobility of capital and the consequent loss of bargaining power of labour unions in countries of both the North and the South. This has happened in the last two to three decades, and is still continuing.

The second contract that has been broken is that of (a) the welfare state in the countries of the North where a set of entitlements and rights of citizens was matched by the responsibilities of the state, and (b) the developmental state in countries of the South.

The third social contract that has been broken is the contract that brought together countries of the South and North in an understanding of living in a common world and, therefore, the mutual responsibility for the project of development. From the Marshall Plan which presaged the beginnings of development assistance to current day discussions of 'aid fatigue' and conditionality is a significant step.

The breaking of these contracts has brought untold hardship for the majority of people in this world because it has resulted in loss of livelihoods, growing insecurity and exclusion of large groups of people from taking part in the social, cultural, political and economic life. However, the breaking of the social contracts also provides windows of opportunity for negotiating the way we will be governed in the future because capitalism cannot operate without regulation. Each of these contracts, overtly for the first two, and less overtly for the third, was a deeply gendered contract. The contract between employers and employees, for example was mainly between *male* workers' unions and public and private sector firms. The needs of women workers, even in nations where the social democratic contract was best developed, were not fully recognized. The welfare state of the North and the development programmes of the South were deeply gendered in terms of what they did not include, that is the responsibilities of the care economy, the rights of mothers, and girls' education.

This re-negotiation, however, cannot happen without women, without recognition of women's political and economic rights as citizens. One of the reasons is because of the growing feminization of labour making women workers numerically at least a force to reckon with. Organizations and unions can no longer afford to re-negotiate the social contract between workers and employers without women. Similarly there is a complete re-thinking on the project of development, although less clearer at this point. However, what has become clear is that, without gender analysis of budgets, without going through how money is allocated for different needs, what happens to the needs of women specifically in these contexts, the rewiring of these social contracts will not happen. The critical issue for gender and development activism is to recognize the changes taking place and to act to secure gender fair and just development.

Why citizenship and what does it mean in development policy and practice?

While the global social contracts cannot be re-negotiated without recognition of women's political and economic rights as citizens, the struggles to re-define the meaning and practice of citizenship in a globalizing world and make this a part of the development policy and practice has become a central agenda.

While citizenship is today a new and emerging concern in development, the concept and practice of citizenship was not something that those working in international development understood or did. This was for a number of reasons not the least of

gender, citizenship and governance

which has to do with the fact that development policy and practice has for a number of decades viewed 'development' as a technical exercise whereas questioning the meaning of citizenship is a political issue entailing the interrogation of why underprivileged groups in society and in particular contexts are not entitled to the same rights and access as powerful groups.

A number of shifts in development practice have led to this re-thinking. First, while the participation of people in determining their own development has been around both as a value and methodology of work for at least the last three decades and has informed the work of many development agencies especially in the non-government sector, it emerged as a key concern in the 1990s with the rise of the 'good governance' agenda in development. The need to build accountability of governance and public institutions and their responsiveness to the differentiated and unequal public that they are supposed to serve meant increasing poor and marginalized peoples' *influence* over wider decision making processes. In other words, peoples' participation as a value and practice emerged from its original context in 'community projects' and assumed significance in terms of the right to political participation (Gaventa and Jones 2002).

Second, in the 1990s a new shift is discernible both in development thought and practice, which brought the development and human rights communities closer together, and this shift is based on a discourse of rights. Development agents have for the most part attempted to draw attention to the problems of poverty and marginalization through 'planned attempts' to analyze and meet peoples' needs through technical means. However, the failure to eliminate poverty and marginalization has led to questioning the 'technical' approach of needs assessment and the assertion that people have a right to development leading to a rights-based approach that politicizes needs. In the human rights field there is a discernible shift from only seeing civic and political rights as the arena of struggle to recognizing the indivisibility of rights and a growing pressure to make social, economic and cultural rights the remit of human rights agendas.

Third, international political developments have also contributed to this re-thinking. The processes of globalization or processes of global restructuring, cultural, economic, political and social processes, have resulted in a *crisis of control* in the world order. No one centre of authority has the ability to manage the changes in a way that will take care of those groups of people who are harmed by the changes. The crisis of control and the negative impacts that the model of development has had on peoples' lives has in turn given rise to global movements for change, as for example, the global justice movements. This phenomenon, termed as global citizen action, no longer limits the struggle for rights to nation-states giving rise to questioning of the concept of citizenship and rights defined narrowly as a 'given' set of entitlements (rights) by virtue of living within or belonging to a territory, a nation.
Nation-states are in crisis as there is a heightened sense of political awareness of ethnic and cultural differences partly due to the ever-increasing international migrations. Added to this is the fact that in many parts of the world nation-states are being fragmented on the basis of politicized differences. Linking citizenship to nation-states has resulted in exclusions that have to be addressed.

Finally, there is growing a crisis of legitimacy in the relationship between citizens and institutions that affect their lives and this is happening the world over and including in the developed nations. The crisis of legitimacy is most evident in the crisis of representational politics as citizens as voters increasingly find themselves unable to exert control over those that they elect to represent them in national parliaments. The Iraq crisis unfolding in 2003 bears testimony to the distance between citizens in Europe and their elected representatives.

Citizenship in liberal thought and common sense

The concept of citizenship as it is understood in liberal political theory, as also in the common sense definitions that we operate with, assumes the existence of a human subject prior to the markings of gender, class, caste, community and other forms of difference and inequality. The rights of the individual are premised on this human core that all individuals are seen to possess. Legal personhood is conferred on the basis of this human core. The law is then seen to be a neutral instrument that confers rights based on this essence. The citizen thus created, who is the bearer of rights and who can act politically to secure more entitlements, is considered to be neutral (i.e. sexless, classless, etc.). This results in two kind of effects: first that it invisibilizes the imprint of social relations that make up the individual; second, it obscures the historical processes through which in any given society, the needs and interests of certain categories of people becomes the norm on which citizenship is based (Mukhopadhyay 1998).

Feminist critiques

Feminist critiques of the liberal notion of citizenship have formed the basis for broadening the concept of citizenship and linking different approaches. These critiques explore the limitations of the equality and equal rights agenda, the liberal tradition of conceptualizing citizenship rights and the tension between equality and difference.

In long periods of history, women have been legally denied rights and privileges enjoyed by men. However, though in most countries women have won the right to vote, legal barriers to female participation in the labour force have been removed, concessions have been made for women's right to hold property in their own name, in real terms, structures of oppression and subordination of women have remained intact. Formal equality does not guaranty structural equality between women and men, and in fact it obscures and legitimizes real inequalities between women and men.

Equal citizenship rights may imply applying equal standards to all citizens. However, in reality it becomes meaningless, if, to begin with different groups of citizens are different and unequal. This has special pertinence to sexual equality. For women to have *equal* right to work, for example, they may actually need *more* than men. They need maternity leave, workplace nurseries, extra safety conditions when pregnant, time off for menstruation, and as long as they remain principally responsible for reproductive labour at home, they need assistance to free them from household labour to enter the labour market equally. To make matters further complex, not all women are equal either. Women of different age, class, caste, ethnicity, race have different social position and power, and therefore different needs.

So what is citizenship and what does it mean for excluded groups?

Lister (1998) refers to citizenship as one of those slippery terms which everyone understands at some level but find difficult to arrive at an agreed definition of. She points out that this is partly because of the different traditions that have informed the debate on citizenship and partly because the way we define citizenship also reflects the social and political community that we want to belong to. According to Lister, citizenship can be understood as both a status, involving rights, and as a practice involving political participation in its broadest sense.

The language of citizenship has been and is constantly being deployed by diverse social movements including women's movements to visibilize and politicize their needs. The meaning of citizenship in feminist politics operates at four dimensions: the political level; the economic level (substantive economic equality is implied in respect to property, labour market and unpaid work); the cultural level of norms and values; and the personal level of family, home and relationships. For citizenship to operate substantively, it must be present and visible at all four dimensions. Thus feminists have been defining and redefining 'citizenship' not in its narrow sense as the 'right to vote', but to mean *entitlements, rights, responsibilities* and *agency* (Gita Sen 2002). The process of the construction of rights has to be imbued with an ethos of *inclusion, equity* and *equality* and it is this process that will help redefine the meaning of nation and citizenship.

What does citizenship look like in practice?

Much of the scholarly work on citizenship tends to be abstract whereas the practice of citizenship involves real people struggling for recognition, rights and inclusion in policy agendas in located situations. Thus it is only by interrogating these experiences that we can arrive at what is involved in citizen action and how these struggles change the meaning of citizenship.

Women's activism over the last three decades for rights, equal treatment and policies that enhance human development and justice for all provide insights into the practice of citizenship. On the one hand, women's constituencies have emerged as global citizens as they have argued for the right to development, freedom from domestic and sexual violence, sexual and reproductive rights, the implementation of CEDAW and the Beijing Platform for Action at international forums. This activism was greatly helped by the international conferences on women, the Population and Development Conference, the Social Summits and the Human Rights conferences, which all provided the space for the articulation of rights and the historical moment to organize around these rights. On the other hand, in each and every single case, it has been necessary to organize from the 'bottom-up', to create awareness at a national and community level and among women themselves that women had a right to have rights. The struggle has been to disentangle a woman's identity as subject/citizen imbued with rights from that of her identity as daughter, sister, wife and mother and in other words the subject of ascribed social relations (Mukhopadhyay 1998).

Global citizen action has been necessary to provide the wider political environment for the construction of new rights whereas the hard work of politicizing needs at a local and national level has involved entrenching these rights. The articulation of rights has given 'voice' to women's demands but it has been necessary to work with powerful institutions to change the rules and demand responsiveness and accountability. This has meant working within the political spaces provided by these institutions and also constructing new political spaces.

A discernible shift in women's activism at national and international level in the struggle to be citizens in their own right is that of the move away from demanding formal equality to insisting on substantive equality. This has had a number of effects. First, it has meant unpacking the homogenous construct 'woman' to using the real experiences of women living at the intersection of caste, class, ethnic and racial disadvantages in the construction of rights. Second, this has in turn meant moving away from feminist orthodoxies that one set of demands for equality are equally applicable to all kinds of women. Third, it has meant challenging the liberal conceptions of citizenship and particularly the public-private split. While the critique of the public-private split has been the basis of feminist scholarship on citizenship, in action this has meant linking private wrongs to political solutions. It has also meant redefining what political participation is and that it is not limited to the formal arena of politics with a big 'P'. It has also challenged the notion that struggle for women's rights, rights of minorities for self-expression, community activism, is not citizenship because it is parochial and it is specific community interests which are being pursued rather than some wider common good.

Finally, feminist politics is learning that the meaning of citizenship, rights of the individual and democracy are not unwavering universalisms based on a human essence that we all enjoy equally. Thus feminist politics and theory needs to move out of an epistemology that maps gender identity on to the model of the humanist subject or citizen/subject to making visible the processes of norming from the point of view of those who are excluded. In this process of exposing the micro-politics of how othering and exclusion takes place democracy needs to be seen as a critical resource rather than as a structural guarantee (Mukhopadhyay 1998).

What does citizenship mean for development policy and practice?

We return to the realization that conventional development efforts to eliminate poverty and inequality have met with limited success because poverty and inequality are most critically about power relations. The technical approach to delivering on poverty and inequality by getting institutions right is only a limited approach. It cannot be kept up without a corresponding pressure from those who are poor, marginalized and excluded on these and other counts. And this is where the development as a right comes in because it politicizes needs, helps create constituencies demanding these rights, responsiveness and accountability.

The struggle to re-define citizenship is important in the context of development for a number of reasons:
- It politicizes 'needs' and has the *potential* to transform marginalized groups from victims and/or passive beneficiaries to agents demanding change.
- It can redefine political participation from being merely that which 'citizens' do in the formal arena of politics (vote, get elected, hold public office) to citizens who 'make and shape' policies (Cornwall and Gaventa 2000: 8).
- It can help to build civil society institutions and give voice to citizen groups.
- It would improve responsiveness and accountability of institutions because the process of building accountability requires putting equal emphasis on the need to build both citizens' capabilities to articulate rights and the capabilities of political and economic institutions to respond and be held to account (Jones and Gaventa 2002).

Governing for equity: lessons learned

What do the case studies represent?

The case studies in this volume represent civil society initiatives to intervene in governance to bring about changes in institutional practices that secure gender strategic interests. Thus the projects are not just about decentralization of government, or about getting more women into government and political office, or about law reform. Rather these themes represent the areas in which the participating organizations have intervened with the objective of reforming and re-writing the 'rules of the game'. In order to change the 'rules of the game' and secure the position and interests of the most marginalized groups of women, it would be necessary to create access to governance institutions, act within these institutions to enable them to respond to women's needs and interests and finally, stake a claim to new entitlements arising from the needs articulated by those affected by lack of rights and influence. This logic formed the basis of the categorization of themes: taking office, engendering governance institutions and claiming citizenship.

Taking office
Gaining access to governance institutions

Claiming citizenship
Staking a claim to entitlements

Engendering governance institutions
Creating responsiveness and accountability

The case studies and what they teach us

The case studies illuminate the *meaning* and *practice* of good governance from a gender perspective.

In their case study, Sakhi, a women's resource centre based in the city of Trivandrum in Kerala state in India, analyze their involvement in the democratic decentralization process underway in Kerala. Constitutional amendments in 1993 paved the way for setting up local self-government institutions in India. The constitutional amendments aimed at: (1) setting up elected local self-government institutions; (2) devolving decision making power for development projects to these bodies; and (3) providing for a 33% quota for women for the elections to local government institutions.

In Kerala, these constitutional amendments paved the way for setting up a unique model of decentralized planning in 1996. Entitled the People's Planning Campaign (PPC), this model devolved both power and funds to local self-government institutions. Thirty five to forty per cent of the state's funds were to be put at the disposal of the local government institutions for spending on projects formulated by them. Participation of the people in setting up priorities and deciding on projects was made a key principle. An important stipulation for the PPC was that a separate chapter in the development report had to be devoted to women's development and that 10% of the budget had to be specifically allocated for women's development.

Decentralization of government is being offered as the panacea to improve governance, make governance transparent and participatory, bring government structures closer to people and therefore more relevant to peoples' lives. Sakhi's experience has helped to debunk many of these myths precisely because these have been interrogated from the point of view of women.

First, since local government is more embedded in local social structures than national government and since prevailing gender ideologies are more concentrated at the local level, it is more difficult for women to penetrate as independent political actors or for them to raise controversial gender issues at this level. The challenge confronting civil society organizations like Sakhi was how to free up this space in order to create political legitimacy and real participation. Sakhi found that they could not address their planned interventions of bringing women's interests to decisions concerning development planning processes without addressing the deeply demeaning ways in women were viewed and treated.

Second, Sakhi's experience highlighted that even where attempts are made to put in place structures for people's participation in local level institutions this does not mean women are taken into account. Procedures were found to be gender neutral and gender blind in decentralized development despite strict guidelines for democratic decision making, women's participation and budgetary allocations. There was the incorrect assumption that women and men have equal power and status and the model of development did not consider the need to transform unequal gender relations.

Third, Sakhi's experience also shows that despite the existence of regulations favouring women's participation in the planning process and budgetary allocations to meet women's priorities, women could not take advantage of these favourable conditions to further their strategic interests. They did not have the organization or the articulation of interests to intervene as agents in the planning process. Sakhi set about remedying this situation by helping women to organize, providing information and training so that women themselves could undertake a needs analysis.

Institutional change and accountability of governance institutions to gender equality were identified as key issues for the programme. But what does it mean to hold institutions accountable to poor women's interests?

The project undertaken by the Aurat Foundation and Shirkat Gah illustrates the importance of carving out spaces for the articulation of interests and shaping the accountability interface between these interests and institutions. Sometimes these are spaces opened up by decision making institutions and at other times political spaces have to be created.

The importance of being extremely strategic, being able to locate the exact point of intervention (as in a specific department, structure, or process), the critical actors, and the moment was evident in the case studies. However, to do this there needs to be transparency, access to information and understanding of institutional practices and procedures.

When the military government formed the National Commission on the Status of Women (NCSW) in Pakistan, civil society groups were doubtful about the mandate, function, and membership of this Commission and whether it could actually perform the role that civil society organizations wanted it to perform. The question facing the two women's rights organizations, Shirkat Gah and the Aurat Foundation, was how to build accountability of this state-sponsored institution to women's strategic interests. Disengagement was not an option nor was it strategic to merely agitate for changes without suggesting what these changes should be. The strategy adopted instead was to involve the members of the Commission, government policymakers in a dialogue with civil society organizations in the country at all levels and also to expose the NCSW members to the experiences of similar bodies from other countries in an international conference. These strategies worked to introduce to the NCSW the real issues facing women that they would have to take care of, built ownership leading to the NCSW itself recommending to government what changes were required in its mission, mandate, and powers in order to better serve women's strategic interests. By holding the post-facto consultation on the role and mandate of the Commission, the Aurat Foundation and Shirgat Gah opened up spaces that were by all accounts closed to public participation.

The case study presented by CALS (Centre for Applied Legal Studies, University of Witwatersrand, South Africa) analyzes its role in the reform of the customary law of marriage under the new constitutional dispensation in South Africa (in line with gender equality and cultural values), and in seeking to ensure the effective implementation of the law (so that it would actually improve the quality of life of women). It sought to assess how effective CALS' method and contribution was to both of these processes, and to draw lessons applicable to similar situations in other countries.

The CALS case study best illustrates the meaning and practice of citizenship from a gender perspective. First, the case study highlights how important it is to insist on the honest representation of the lived experience of specific categories of women (the most marginalized or those who are most affected by the specific lack of rights) in constructing substantive citizenship as against citizenship as formal rights. As for example, in the reform of customary law on marriage in South Africa, CALS established the need to have women's experience and needs as their reference point. For this reason they de-emphasized the issue of polygyny because for the women living under customary law this was not the most important problem. Far more important for the women was to establish the right to marital property, custody of children and not to be seen as legal minors. Feminists have always held monogamy to be the cornerstone of feminist demands for equality between men and women in marriage. CALS argued that to outlaw polygyny legally would not necessarily have the desired effect in practice and in fact deprive women who were presently living in polygynous unions to legal protection. A much more pragmatic approach, and one that was adopted in the reform, was to insist on those provisions that make polygyny even more expensive than it is now, ensuring thereby its demise.

Second, in the practice of citizenship the importance of creating 'voice' for women's concerns is paramount. The research undertaken by CALS to identify the practices, needs and interests of women in relation to marriage gave voice to women's concerns in the law reform process. Third, articulating 'voice' does not necessarily lead to better outcomes for women. The case study highlights the significance of ensuring that this 'voice' reaches the institutions that affect the lives of citizens, that changes take place and that there is an accountability interface. CALS tried to do this at every stage of the law reform process starting from written submission to South Africa Legal Commission, contributing to the Issue Paper, speaking to women in Parliament before the Bill was tabled, briefing the Committee after the tabling of the Bill, participating in the public hearings on the Bill, identifying different categories of problems of implementation after the Bill was passed and communicating this to the appropriate authorities, and reviewing implementation and especially the role of officials responsible for implementing the Act.

Sister Namibia campaigned for equal representation of women in political office. Formal representation by women as a disadvantaged group was seen as a way of guaranteeing them more equal weight, and to counteract the balance of power of the dominant groupings that tend to be represented in elected office. Their arguments did not rest on notions of group representation, but made the point that assemblies would be enriched by a wider range of opinions, knowledge and concerns. Whether these women represent women or not, the case for increasing numbers of women still stood. To have one's voice heard was seen as a basic entitlement of those governed. In the process of undertaking this campaign Sister Namibia spearheaded the formation of a women's organization, the Namibian Women's Manifesto Network (NWMN), and has contributed to a more robust civil society in Namibia, one that includes women's rights on its agenda. On the question of women's political participation Sister Namibia was concerned that current levels of women's participation were not satisfactory at national and regional levels, and that given the imminent changes to the electoral system at local level the high proportion of women at local level would not be sustained.

In September 2000 Sister Namibia and the NWMN took up the 50/50 Campaign in earnest, with the aim of building women's organization, raising awareness of their rights as citizens and political actors, making the issue of women's equal participation a political issue. At the same time the campaign raised the awareness of public and state actors of the importance of women's increased political participation. A broad range of Namibians were engaged on the issue through meetings, the media, marches in small towns and in the capital city Windhoek.

Never before was there such widespread mobilization on a women's issue. The campaign resulted in widespread awareness of women's political participation. It brought women together across their diversities. Strategies were a combination of grass-roots organizing, mobilization of media, drawing on research and legal skills, bringing NGOs and women's groups together in local and national consultations, and in marches. While legal specialists had helped to draw up a Bill for equal representation of women and men at all levels of government, the campaign took this Bill to all constituencies of women for discussion and debate so that it not only became a tool for raising awareness but also a method to draw in ordinary women into the process of law reform.

The campaign generated widespread discussion throughout Namibia. While it is realized that the goal is unreachable in the short-term, the campaign has raised awareness on the issue of women's participation in political office, and has enhanced the visibility of women in office.

Defining good governance from a gender perspective

We began the Gender, Citizenship and Governance programme with the intention to contribute to the generation of knowledge and practice that would help to make gender equity and equality a core concern in the debate on and practice of good governance. The participating organizations and their action research projects provided the empirical ground arriving at definitions of good governance from a gender perspective. Definitions operate at the level of meaning and practice.

The meaning of good governance from a gender perspective

We found that the meaning of women taking political office signified not only the creation of mechanisms for their entry into public office but also establishing women as legitimate political actors (as opposed to private persons who do not have a place in politics and the public sphere).

Engendering governance institutions meant building accountability of governance institutions to women as citizens, changing rules, procedures and priorities that exclude the participation of poor women and the incorporation of their interests in the development agenda, and the mobilization and organization of women's voice in civil society.

What does citizenship mean for poor women? First, it meant the right to participate and to be agents. The meaning of citizenship for those groups who are on the margins of society is centrally about acquiring the power to define the problem of lack of rights and the solutions that would ameliorate this condition. Second, it meant aspiring for realizing substantive equality as opposed to formal equality. The case studies highlight how important it is to insist on the honest representation of the lived experience of specific categories of women (the most marginalized or those who are most affected by the specific lack of rights) in constructing substantive citizenship as against citizenship as formal rights.

The practice of good governance

Constructing voice
Women's voice and women's organization as a political constituency within civil society are crucial in order to break through the barriers that restrict their participation in politics, within governance institutions and their claims to citizenship. The projects helped to articulate specific women's voices, those of the most marginalized by foregrounding the real experiences of exclusion from entitlements and rights that these women face.

Creating communities of struggle
The case studies highlighted the important role of a political constituency of women in building awareness in civil society and creating a public broadly sympathetic to the principle of gender equality, and challenging prevailing notions of women's subordination. In order to give 'voice' to women's demands an immense amount of work has to take place to organize and mobilize constituencies that grow into an awareness of the right to have a right, and the right to participate in decisions affecting their life.

Shaping the accountability interface
Articulating 'voice' does not necessarily lead to better outcomes for women. The case studies highlight the significance of ensuring that this 'voice' reaches the institutions that affect the lives of citizens, that changes take place and that there is an accountability interface.

Carving out space
The projects also demonstrated the importance of carving out spaces for the articulation of interests and shaping the accountability interface between these interests and institutions. Sometimes these are spaces opened up by decision making institutions and at other times political spaces have to be created. The projects used constructed spaces, created spaces, and opened up spaces that were by all accounts closed to public participation.

Working on both sides / in and out of the state

All the case studies highlight the importance of citizen voice and constituting women as a political force, in order to shift and reshape institutional agendas, rules and practices. The task is twofold: on the one hand getting women more aware of their rights and more aware of how to hold institutions to account, and on the other intervening in organizational processes to reshape how organizations function. Most of the projects worked in tandem with state institutions sometimes aligning with the state and other times agitating for changes.

Establishing authority

In all cases the NGOs concerned were able to engage with civil society and state actors in the ways they did because of the legitimacy and authority they had established as a result of the contributions through their work.

Demystifying institutions

The case studies highlight the importance of demystifying institutions in order to enhance responsiveness. Looking at institutions from the perspective of poor, marginalized women raised issues of broader institutional accountability, that institutions are not accountable to poor men also, and that there is often a lack of transparency. Hence redressing these imbalances from the point of poor women will result in better institutional accountability to all.

References

Cornwall, A. and J. Gaventa, 'From users and choosers to makers and shapers: repositioning participation in social policy', *IDS Bulletin*, vol. 31, no 4 (2000), pp. 50-62.

Jones, E. and J. Gaventa, 'Concepts of citizenship: a review'. Development Bibliography 19. Sussex, Institute of Development Studies, 2002.

Lister, R., 'Citizen in action: citizenship and community development in Northern Ireland context'. *Community Development Journal*, vol. 33, no. 3 (1998), pp. 226-35.

Mukhopadhyay, M., *Legally dispossessed: gender, identity and the process of law*. Calcutta, Stree, 1998.

Sen, G., 'Feminist Politics in a fundamentalist world' Key-note speech. In: M. Mukhopadhyay (ed.) *Governing for equity: gender, citizenship and governance*. Amsterdam, KIT, 2002.

introduction

27

Good governance from a gender perspective

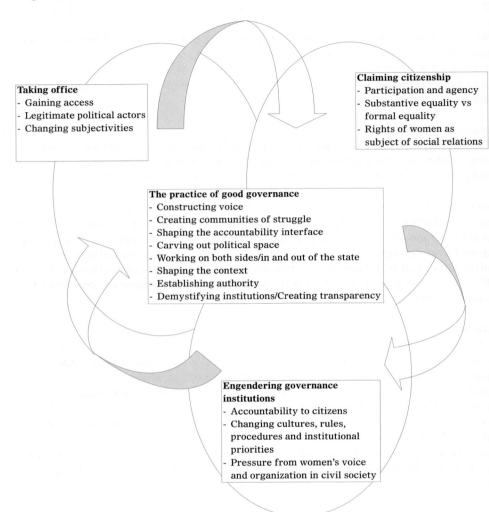

Taking office
- Gaining access
- Legitimate political actors
- Changing subjectivities

Claiming citizenship
- Participation and agency
- Substantive equality vs formal equality
- Rights of women as subject of social relations

The practice of good governance
- Constructing voice
- Creating communities of struggle
- Shaping the accountability interface
- Carving out political space
- Working on both sides/in and out of the state
- Shaping the context
- Establishing authority
- Demystifying institutions/Creating transparency

Engendering governance institutions
- Accountability to citizens
- Changing cultures, rules, procedures and institutional priorities
- Pressure from women's voice and organization in civil society

Aleyamma Vijayan

Decentralization process and women: the case of Kerala, India

Kerala is one of the 28 states that make up the Indian Union. It is situated in the southern most tip of the Indian sub-continent. The state accounted for 3.1% of India's population and 1.2% of its land area in 2001 (Government of India 2003). Kerala stands apart from other Indian states because of its high human development measured in terms of life expectancy, low infant mortality rate and literacy rates (Appendix). The quality of life indicators put Kerala closer to high-income, developed countries than to the rest of India or its counterparts in the low-income world, despite its poor economic status. But Kerala's achievements in the social sector do not go hand in hand with its progress in material production sectors. There is severe crisis in the productive sectors and overburdening of the fragile ecological system. There is economic stagnation, increasing unemployment and falling per capita income.

Women in Kerala have achieved parity to men with respect to literacy levels and this has been true for almost two decades now. The recent 2001 census indicates that the literacy rates for women were about 88% as against 94% for men (Government of India 2003). The age at marriage for men and women in Kerala has always been consistently higher than the national average. The state's excellent gender development indicators are also clouded with contrasts. The gender paradox is more visible when we take into account the work participation of women, which is lower than the national average and which has also tended to decline. An important reason for this decline is the severe unemployment rate in the state (Isaac et al 1999). The level of unemployment is higher among women than men in both rural and urban areas.

The social status of women in this state is considered to be high as a consequence of matriliny being practised among some communities and due to the higher educational level. Yet this is not reflected in the political participation as one would expect and here Kerala reflects the trend in the country with the participation rate of women in state legislature bodies less than 10%. Kerala also has the distinction of being one of the few states in India with overall sex ratio favouring women. Yet according to the last census, the sex ratio in the age group 0-6 years shows a trend unfavourable to the girl child being 963 girls for every 1000 boys (Government of India 2003).

Another paradox is the increase in violence against women. According to the data of Crime Records Bureau in 1991, reported cases of violence against women in the state were 1867. However, this has multiplied to reach 7306 cases in 1997. Another multi-site survey of domestic violence in seven sites in India during 1997-99 indicated that Trivandrum (the capital city of Kerala state) had the highest levels of violence

decentralization process

reported (63.5%) among urban non-slum sites. The overall level of physical violence in Kerala was about 25.9% (Domestic violence in India 2000).

Process of political decentralization in India

India has been a successful parliamentary democracy for the past five decades. The Union Government with its headquarters in the nation's capital, New Delhi, and the federated States were for a long time the major governing institutions as determined by the provisions of the Indian Constitution. However in 1993, the 73rd and 74th amendments to the Constitution was passed making Local Self Governing Institutions (LSGIs) mandatory as part of government. A uniform 3-tier system came into formal existence: district; *taluk/block* (a cluster of villages); and village level in the rural areas and Municipalities and Corporations in large urban centres. These elected local bodies have a 5-year term and, in the event of dissolution, elections must be held within six months. An important aspect of the amendment was that one-third of the seats in at all levels of local government was reserved for the election of women.

All state governments had to appoint finance commissions to decide on the sharing of revenue between the state government and the LSGIs. A separate 11th schedule was added to the Constitution, listing 29 subjects that could be devolved to the local bodies. However, Article 243G of the Constitution mandated the state governments to decide on devolving powers and functions to the local bodies.

Decentralization in Kerala

> *One of the first decisions made by the Left Democratic Government (LDF) elected to power in 1996 was to earmark 35 to 40% of the outlay of the Ninth Five Year Plan towards projects and programmes to be drawn up by the Local Self Government Institutions. (Isaac et al 1999)*

In 1994, the Kerala Government amended the Panchayat Raj[1] Act in line with the constitutional amendment. Kerala was one of the few states that devolved functions, finances and functionaries to make the *panchayats* real institutions of local self-government.

A distinctive feature of the decentralization experiment in Kerala is its insistence on mass participation and transparency. To this effect, a revolutionary experiment of power sharing, the People's Planning Campaign (PPC), was launched formally in Kerala on 17 August 1996 to formulate the 9th Plan in a participatory way. The PPC was introduced as a means to overcome the problems of Kerala's development crisis. The campaign was an attempt to operationalize, conceptualize and institutionalize a system of multilevel, people centred planning process suitable to the regional specifications of Kerala (Government of Kerala 2000).

The decentralization process in Kerala was different from what happened elsewhere because:
- Popular participation was given prime importance in identifying needs and formulating plan proposals. The decentralization process was seen as a people's

ovement whereby they establish their role in designing and planning development
terventions. A campaign mode was adopted to popularize the idea. Maximum
popular participation was ensured at every stage of planning process. A bottom–up,
participatory, scientific and transparent process for local planning was initiated.
- 35-40% of the state's Plan Funds were devolved for projects/schemes to be
  formulated and to be implemented by LSGIs. All government Departmental
  Schemes were to be implemented in consultation with them. Local bodies were
  given powers to call for help from experts and technical people to prepare and
  prioritise a list of projects.
- The State Government of Kerala initiated steps for administrative re-organization
  and statutory change in order to institutionalize the process of local level planning
  and implementation by setting up an administrative reforms committee. According
  to their report, necessary staff was deployed and powers devolved to make the local
  bodies truly LSGIs.
- At every phase, gender was integrated into the planning process. Out of the 35-40%
  funds allotted to the panchayats, it was mandatory to spend 10% exclusively on
  projects for women.

Hence the uniqueness of the model was that the Government did not wait for certain
pre-conditions, such as building up of the administrative capacity and structures,
before functions and powers were transferred to LSGIs. While the process was taking
place, the necessary training was organized to build the capacity of local bodies. An
information base was created and linkages between various agencies and
departments were established.

Gender issues in decentralized governance: the case of Sakhi

Sakhi, a resource centre for women, is based in Trivandrum, the capital city of
Kerala, and it came into being in 1996. Sakhi's long-term objective is to contribute to
the establishment of a society free from discrimination and exploitation based on
caste, class and gender. Sakhi is a feminist organization which aims to mainstream
gender into the political discourse of Kerala. It believes that governance is an area to
which women's organizations should pay special attention because conscious and
purposive intervention are needed to ensure the development of gender aware
policies and programmes for equity in governance. Women's involvement in politics is
crucial in the context of emerging issues of globalization and internal structural
transformation, the changing nature of nationalism and the rise in religious
fundamentalism. Sakhi believes that every issue has to be analyzed from a multi-
cultural and gender perspective. Women, who live in deeply gendered institutions, are
the worst hit by the fast changing and violent global forces. Women's capabilities
need to be enhanced to analyze such issues through the prism of their own
experiences and genuine needs of society.

The programme

Sakhi has been associated with the People's Planning Campaign right from its
inception. Being a feminist organization, Sakhi analyzed the decentralization process
underway in Kerala from a gender perspective. The major goal thus was to intervene

in the decentralized planning process so as to make gender concerns central to the decision making regarding allocation of resources and to secure practical and strategic gender interests through planning.

In pursuance of the above goal, Sakhi undertook an action research programme with the following broad objectives:
- Understanding the aim and process of decentralization of governance in Kerala and to study the way in which power and privileges are shared and livelihoods and basic human rights are insured. From this study and discussions with experts, the objective was to evolve some criteria for good governance.
- In this context, understanding the process of whether and how governance is gendered. What are the obstacles and hurdles in the process?
- Documenting the experiences of elected women representatives and assess how far their participation in the public realm enabled them to bring gender issues to the centre-stage of politics.
- Undertaking capacity building of elected women so that an empowered constituency is created to carry on the gender advocacy effectively.

The focus of the research was to map the structures, players and processes through which decentralized planning addresses gender strategic interests.

To achieve this, the following activities were undertaken:
1. Work closely with two panchayats by
   - attending meetings of (a) elected representatives; (b) grama sabhas (ward level gathering of people a minimum of three times a year to identify needs and propose projects); (c) neighbourhood groups (NHGs) or self-help groups (SHGs) which are regular forums in which the process of need identification happens;
   - active involvement in the task force (sectoral committee) on women to influence projects of the Women's Component Plan.
2. Interact with elected representatives
   - to assess how the State-sponsored training programmes helped them;
   - to facilitate a process of change in their understanding of gender issues.
3. Motivate activities with focus on three areas: livelihood issues, health issues and violence against women.
4. Advocacy at broader level on issues of citizenship, gender and governance.

For the purpose of anonymity, the selected panchayats are named as panchayat C and panchayat D. Panchayat C is situated in the coastal area of Kerala where poverty is widespread, there is more illiteracy, the health problems are more acute, and infrastructure is poorly developed. Panchayat D is more akin to the standard Kerala panchayats which have both rural and urban characteristics, where the general literacy level is higher, infrastructure is better developed and where poverty is less acute than the coastal area.

The activities undertaken by Sakhi in the two panchayats can grouped as follows: (1) direct involvement and intervention in the planning process with a view to prioritizing women's needs, formulating projects which are viable and sustainable and contribute to the above mentioned objectives; (2) training for both men and women on gender awareness training and exchange programmes for elected women and on practical skills for women's self-help groups on income generation; (3) undertaking studies and surveys to ascertain women's development needs with a view to informing the planning process; and (4) technical support to set-up vigilance committees for violence against women.

Lessons learned about the planning process

A detailed ethnography of the planning processes undertaken in both panchayats has been developed. A gender analysis of budgetary allocations made in both panchayats is also available. What follows is a summary of main issues and learning related to influencing budgetary allocations for generating livelihoods for women, for women's health issues and for programmes to resist violence against women.

Development reports

The development reports should provide the blue print for the formulation of plans. The chapter on women's development is based not on an analysis of women's position and the problems they face in development. Rather, it is based on commonly held prejudices and assumptions about women that are derogatory and reinforce women's inferiority. As a result, project ideas do not reflect the priorities for women's development at the local level.

Gram sabhas

The *gram sabha*, or village meeting, is the cornerstone of participatory democracy. A number of gram sabhas were held in the two panchayats in 2001 and 2002 to formulate projects, to prioritize and then to finalize projects. A number of problems were observed in the participatory process that undermine the concept of decentralized planning and specifically the integration of gender issues in planning. The first issue has to do with the quantity of participation. The number of people attending the gram sabhas has been dwindling. This trend has two main characteristics. Very few men as compared to women attended these meetings. More poor women attended because they are often the direct beneficiaries of individual projects. Further, the social groups in the village/ward who do not stand to benefit from panchayat budget allocations, for example the middle-class, stayed away almost as if village development was not their concern. This has led some panchayat committee leaders (elected representatives) to declare that these meetings are held only because the government has stipulated that it is a procedure.

The second issue is the quality of participation and this is most evident in the discussions regarding women's development. On the one hand, there is a general lack of ideas for projects that would benefit women's development. In the absence of an analysis of women's concerns and the poor representation of women's interests, there is no coherent articulation of project ideas. On the other hand, the ideas that are put forward are generally those that might provide women with an income in the short run. Projects that help women's livelihoods in a sustained way or address their health and other strategic interests do not feature in the discussions. Sakhi's experience has been that they were invited to give ideas and the suggestions were welcomed.

The third issue is whether the project ideas put forward or worked on in one gram sabha will get followed up through the sectoral committees, the panchayat committee and appear in the plan and budget allocations. This is most noticeable with the women's component of the plan although not limited to it. In the initial gram sabhas, a mix of projects, income generation and those that address women's health and welfare needs, were suggested by Sakhi and enthusiastically taken up. However, the projects that were retained through their passage from project ideas to plans were mainly those that would provide some women short-term income-generation activities. Although the budget allocation for projects other than income-generation did increase in both panchayats, most were dropped.

Sectoral committees
These committees are set up to formulate the projects. The setting up of at least three sectoral committees is mandatory and one of these is the women's component plan committee. Since it is stipulated that an elected woman must head this committee, in both panchayats a woman heads this committee. However, women-headed committee are limited to women's welfare, education and drinking water. None of the elected women have been invited to head committees for industries, fisheries or agriculture.

The formulation of projects for the women's plan is hostage to two considerations. First, projects for women's development have been equated with income generation. Secondly, this is limited to traditional activities with little consideration for developing the technical and marketing possibilities that are necessary to make them sustainable. In both panchayats, introduction of non-traditional activities, feasibility studies and marketing involved prolonged battles between women and the researche on the one hand, and men on the other.

Panchayat committee
This committee is comprised of the elected members that meet regularly to decide on all matters of the panchayat. The sectoral plans are also presented for discussion before being presented to the people at the development seminar. Decision making regarding projects in the two panchayat committees is hostage to gender power relations. For example:
- In panchayat A where the President was a man and the secretary (government official) a woman, the latter was ridiculed on more than one occasion, leading to a reprimand to the President. The Sakhi researcher was approached by the opposition group members to write this up as a form of sexual harassment.
- Only two of the women among seven in panchayat A were vocal, the others were silent most of the time. Three women were observed never to have said anything in 12 successive meetings. Similarly in panchayat B, three out of the six women spoke at the meetings and the others remained silent. The women were intimidated and, therefore, could not speak up.
- In panchayat B as opposed to A, the President was a woman and the secretary (government official) a man. The secretary took on the main role in the discussions and talked mostly to the men present. The secretary has since changed and a woman has taken over making this an all woman-headed panchayat.
- The women sat together in both panchayats at one corner of the table.

Male members taunted the women, particularly if they discussed amongst themselves.

How Sakhi helped the panchayats

Sakhi undertook a number of activities to help the panchayats to function as democratic self-governing institutions.

Training

Training in gender awareness for panchayat committee members
Gender power relations play an important role in the decision making process in the panchayat both because elected women feel powerless, and because decisions on what is an appropriate women's project is based on the 'proper role' of women as perceived by men. Sakhi organized a number of gender-training programmes for all the representatives of the panchayat. The first day of the training was for the male members of the panchayat and the women were asked to join only on the second day. Sakhi observes that these training workshop allowed men to talk about gender issues for the first time, get acquainted with the women members' perspective and since all of this was happening in a non-confrontational and non-threatening atmosphere, men conceded that it was time for a change. Numerous suggestions were proposed to make the panchayat more women-friendly, some of which are already being implemented. One of the issues focused on at subsequent meetings was the construction of masculinity in Kerala society which helped the men to think through their own attitudes towards man/woman relationships.

Training elected women
Women elected to political office face a number of problems, including their insecurity and unawareness about women's issues that they should profile in their political work. As part of Sakhi's plan to form a Network for Elected Women Representatives of Trivandrum District, monthly one-day training sessions are held with the elected women where women's issues are discussed, public speaking and representation is taught, project ideas developed.

self-help groups
The self-help groups are being set up all over the state as part of the plan to organize women to facilitate their development. Since these groups began as thrift and credit groups through which the panchayats can channel the funds for women's development, their ability to articulate women's needs and priorities can in the long run improve gender planning at panchayat level. Towards this end, Sakhi has begun to organize training programmes to focus on social issues rather than on economic issues only. Also, these groups have been exposed to technical training for small-scale industrial projects.

Surveys and studies

Surveys and studies have been undertaken to ascertain women's development needs with a view to informing the planning process. Two kinds of studies and surveys have

decentralization process

been undertaken. The first is a survey of elected women in the two panchayats. The objective was to build a profile of these women, to understand their political aspirations and the difficulties they face as women in performing their public role. The other survey is to ascertain the position of women in the two panchayats. This was undertaken at the request of the panchayats who had been instructed by the State Planning Board that they have to compile this data in order to improve planning. Sakhi agreed to undertake the survey on two aspects: health and violence.

Lessons learned from Sakhi's interventions

The following lessons were learned and provide clues to the ways forward.

Adequate democratic procedures do not automatically promote democracy in gender relations

Central to the process of decentralized planning is the notion of democratic decision making. Priorities have to be agreed by the community at large, looked into by the sectoral committees. The projects proposed need to meet these priorities and to be presented at the development seminar attended by the larger community. Budgets have to be allocated, and the panchayat committee has to approve and finalize the projects for funding. The procedures to enable this level of participation are all in place. All of these structures to ensure democratic participation come with specific guidelines from the State Planning Board regarding women's participation and specific budgetary allocation for women's development. Despite the existing procedures to promote democratic decision making this in itself does not guarantee democracy where gender relations are concerned. The procedures are gender neutral in that they assume that women and men have equal power and status to be authoritative about what should be done. Further, they are gender-blind because the procedures in themselves do not uphold a model or vision of society and development that is gender-fair or based on the transformation of gender relations.

Gender power relations affect decision making processes at the level of committees

Sakhi's involvement in the day-to-day activities and in the planning process undertaken by the panchayats shows that gender power relations play an important role in the decision making process in the panchayat both because elected women feel powerless, and because decisions on what is an appropriate women's project is based on the 'proper role' of women as perceived by men. We learned that there has to be sustained effort to improve unequal power relations, both by efforts to empower elected women members of the committees and by initiating a dialogue with male members about gender relations and making more equitable relations their responsibility.

What is women's development?

In trying to secure practical and strategic gender interests through planning, we have learned that a major obstacle is the *way* in which women's development is conceived. First, there is an equation of women's development projects with income generation. The analysis of budget allocations reveals that the money for women's development was either allocated to income generation projects which are not sustainable, or to women's welfare handouts or a smaller proportion for nutrition and education for pre-school children and pregnant and lactating mothers. Non-traditional employment generation schemes were shunned because of the problem of technical expertise and lack of forward and backward linkages. The mandatory procedures for allocation reinforce this tendency. There is very little freedom to earmark funds for activities like the collection of gender-disaggregated data, awareness building programmes, intervention on health and violence issues. Second, general notions about the proper role of women and propriety in man-woman relations shape the ideas about what is proper women's development project.

The role of elected women representatives

In order to improve planning to make gender concerns central to the decision making regarding allocation of resources, the role of the elected women representatives is crucial. They should be able to uphold women's interests and take forward a strategic gender agenda. For this reason, it is very important to invest in building their capacity to be able to facilitate discussions in the gram sabha and to be able to carry this through the different committees. This should not be a one-time training but an ongoing process, both by the state and the respective political parties.

The critical need for a collective of women

Better articulation of women's needs can only take place if there is a growing demand from women themselves regarding their needs and interests. The formation of self-help groups provides this possibility but only if these groups are exposed to social and development issues and are able to organize themselves as pressure groups. This is also the case for elected women representatives. These women are divided strongly across party lines in Kerala and do not perceive a common identity. They are in politics due to the quota system for women and their political perspectives and analysis needs to be nurtured and facilitated. Their gender perspectives have to be strengthened so as to counter patriarchal structures of the parties and institutions of government.

Ghettoization of women's issues

The political quota (33%) and Women's Component Plan (WCP) in the budget is leading to the 'ghettoization' of women's issues. Women's issues are not considered political issues and the feeling is that since women have 10% of the total budget earmarked for the WCP, this should be enough to deal with all their problems. Conscious efforts have to be made to change this thinking and to make the polity understand that this is a proactive step to correct past anomalies and the WCP is over and above the general fund allocation.

The crisis of the production sector

As has been mentioned above, the state of Kerala is very poor and has a stagnant economy while, at the same time, enjoying high human development indicators. The

decentralization process

37

problems of investing in the productive sector through the money available to the local government bodies exemplify, in microcosm, the overall problems of investmen in production. While funds are available for disbursement to self-help groups for income- generation projects, the absorption capacity is limited. In order to build sustainable livelihoods, much better overall economic planning needs to take place. This would require feasibility and market studies, investment in non- traditional occupations, training and marketing.

The limited power of local self-government institutions

As more and more economic decisions are influenced and controlled by international financial institutions and the state is withdrawing from welfare sectors on the guise of structural adjustment programmes, the limited power of LSGIs becomes clear. Since they are the lowest level of governance and very close to people, they have to face the annoyance of people. The LSGIs need to have more powers over the natural resource base on which the people depend on for their livelihood.

Conclusion

The democratic decentralization is a right step in the right direction but this is not a sufficient step to really decentralize power and democratize decision making processes. Just putting institutions and systems in place is not going to change gende relations and hierarchies of power. This will require very concrete steps to change mindsets and attitudes to empower and strengthen women.

Notes

1 Panchayati Raj is the term used in most Indian languages to mean the local self-government body a the village level.

References

'Beyond the malestream: feminist perspectives on political restructuring and social transformation'. Report of the South Asia regional workshop, 19-31 August 1998, Bangalore, India. Development Alternatives with Women for a New Area (DAWN), 1998.

Chandrasekhar, C.P., 'Democratic decentralization and the planning principle'. Paper presented at the International Conference on Democratic Decentralization, Thiruvananthapuram, Kerala, India, 23-2 May 2000.

Domestic violence in India: a summary report of a multi-site household survey. International Centre for Research on Women (ICRW) and the Centre for Development and Population Activities (CEDPA 2000. URL: http://www.icrw.org/docs/DomesticViolence3.pdf

Government of India. Census of India 2001. New Delhi. URL: http://www.censusindia.net/

Government of Kerala. 'Local self-government'. In: *Economic Review* 1999. Thiruvananthapuram, Sta Planning Board, 2000.

Gurukkal, Rajan, 'Coalition of conflicting interests and the politics of decentralization'. Paper presented at the International Conference on Democratic Decentralization, Thiruvananthapuram, Kerala, India, 23-28 May 2000.

saac, T.M. Thomas, and Richard W. Franke, *Local democracy and development: people's campaign for decentralized planning in Kerala*. New Delhi, Leftword, 2001.

agjeevan, N., N. Ramakantan, 'Grama sabhas'. Paper presented at the International Conference on Democratic Decentralization, Thiruvananthapuram, Kerala, India, 23-28 May 2000.

Muraleedharan, K., 'Dynamics of women's participation in development'. Paper presented at the International Conference on Democratic Decentralization, Thiruvananthapuram, Kerala, India, 23-28 May 2000.

Seema, T.N. and Vanitha Nayak Mukherjee, 'Gender, governance and citizenship in decentralized planning: the experience of people's campaign in Kerala'. 1999.

Tornquist, Olle, 'Of new popular politics of development'. Paper presented at the International Conference on Democratic Decentralization, Thiruvananthapuram, Kerala, India, 23-28 May 2000.

Appendix   **Socioeconomic scenario of Kerala State, 2001**

Area	38,863 Sq.kms
Districts	14
Total Population	31,838,619
Male	15,468,664
Female	16,369,955
Rural population	73%
Urban Population	27%
Female sex ratio-per 1000 males	1058
Density of population (per Esq.)	819 persons
Literacy (excluding 0-6 population)	90.92%
Male	94.20%
Female	87.86%
Life expectancy	
Male	71
Female	75
Age at marriage	
Male	27.19 years
Female	21.85 years
Infant Mortality rate	14 per 1000 live births
Maternal mortality rate	1 per 1000
School enrollment (10-14 age group of girls	84%
Work participation	
Male	47.58
Female	15.85

Source: Government of India. Census of India 2001. URL: http://www.censusindia.net/

Naeem Mirza

Engendering institutions in Pakistan

A dream came true for many in the women's rights movement in Pakistan when the military government announced the formation of a permanent National Commission on the Status of Women (NCSW) in July 2000. But soon the jubilation was marred by the sadness of the fact that there were many colours missing in the rainbow. The Commission, so ardently longed and struggled for by women's organizations and activists, did not appear to have a truly independent or autonomous status, and it lacked a clear mandate. It also became quickly apparent that the NCSW had been arbitrarily constituted without any serious homework and without any consultative process with civil society organizations (CSOs). Would a 'toothless' Commission be able to deliver in the interest of women? An effort to make the Commission stronger and more effective became a major concern at this point for some women's rights groups, and eventually led to the birth of this project, supported by two women's organizations, and the initiation of a civil society initiative to strengthen the Commission. The experiences of these two organizations, Shirkat Gah and the Aurat Foundation, provide insight into the complexities of this civil society initiative to engender the formation and functioning of a national machinery for women, in itself an institution for engendering governance. Beyond providing a useful reflection on the debates and dilemmas surrounding national machinery in general, this project demonstrates the success of a strategy to engage, involve and enhance 'stakeholdership' of an initially hostile constituency.

The United Nations (UN) defines a national machinery for women as: 'a single body or complex organized system of bodies, often under different authorities, but recognized by the government as the institution dealing with the promotion of the status of women[1].' The project of Shirkat Gah and the Aurat Foundation is unique in that it took up the challenge created by a difficult situation and, through a very strategic process, managed to mainstream civil society concerns into the state machinery itself through collective processes of learning and sharing. The experiences of Shirkat Gah and the Aurat Foundation demonstrate the challenges and highlight the nuances of the process of setting up a machinery which is adequately responsive to the community women for whose welfare it has been set up and yet has enough political authority to hold the entire government accountable for advancing gender equality. At the same time, the achievements of their post-facto intervention demonstrate the significance of civil society engagement with the government system, despite its obvious flaws.

Background to the project

A key demand of women's organizations in Pakistan has been for the establishment of a permanent commission on the status of women to address the inequality of women's status and rights. The demand has been made since 1976 and periodically reiterated as a recommendation in civil society and government documents until 1998. The demand gained momentum in the build-up to the Fourth World Conference on Women and was recommended in several chapters of the Pakistan National Report that was prepared jointly by the government and civil society. The recommendations were repeated in the Ninth Five Year Plan and the last Commission of Inquiry on Women (1997) as well as the National Plan of Action for Women (1998).

The Beijing Platform for Action[2] added a new focus to the role of national machinerie '(it) is the central policy coordinating-unit inside government. Its main task is to support government-wide mainstreaming of gender-equality perspective in all policy areas' (Para 201, IV, H). This is particularly in order that '… before decisions are taken, an analysis is made of the effects on women and men' (Para 202, IV, H). As such, the national machinery for women is mandated to engender the functioning of the state through oversight and advisory functions. However, this body is usually constituted by the state, and the state itself may have limited perspective on gender to begin with. As Naila Kabeer (1994) points out, 'both conscious interest politics as well as unconscious bias may play a role in policy 'framing''. This was indeed the complex situation in which the women's organizations of Pakistan found themselves.

The specific context of Pakistan at the point of initiation of this project was that Parliament had been suspended and a military government was in power. While a number of institutional reforms were being initiated by the military government to increase accountability and transparency in government, and representatives of CSO were being invited to lead important policymaking bodies, there was a dilemma about being associated with such a non-democratic government. As Goetz (2002) pointed out:

> Many states are currently making considerable efforts to augment dialogue and consultation between state actors and women in civil society, and also to increase th numbers of women within public institutions. … But these opportunities for 'dialogue' do not provide women with legally actionable rights to demand answers from public officials … nor even with the basic information about decision making and policy implementation which is needed in order to assess whether official commitments to gender equity or poverty reduction are being implemented proper

However, Shirkat Gah and the Aurat Foundation felt that, while maintaining some distance from the state, the opportunities should be used to influence governance by pursuing the agenda of a national institution for the advancement of women. As a long-term measure, keeping in mind the prospect of restoration of democracy, all political parties and a collective of CSOs should be part of this demand so that it was firmly embedded in the political agenda and yet drew strength from the women's movement.

However, the military government of General Musharraf pre-empted this by abrupt setting up the Pakistan National Commission on the Status of Women in July 2000 without any transparent process or consultation. Critical lacunae remained relating structure, mandate and powers of the NCSW, since it did not appear to have a truly

ndependent or autonomous status, legitimate enforcing authority or clear mandate.
The CSOs were apprehensive that it might be unable to make any significant
contribution towards changing the situation of women.

Experiences of the project

The Aurat ('Woman') Publication and Information Service Foundation is a national
organization, established in 1986 as a civil society organization committed to women's
empowerment in society. Working in all four provinces and almost all 100 districts of
Pakistan, the Aurat Foundation's overall goal is to develop an enabling environment
for women's empowerment at all levels through participatory democracy and good
governance in Pakistan; through enabling women to acquire greater control over
knowledge, resources and institutions; and through developing and strengthening
networks of CSOs. Shirkat Gah Women's Resource Centre was established in 1975 and
is today working in all four provinces of Pakistan. It has a vision of 'fully empowered
women in a just and vibrant, democratic and tolerant and environmentally sound
society, where equity and opportunity are ensured for all, resources sustainably used,
where peace prevails and where the state is responsive.' Shirkat Gah combines
advocacy and capacity building based on research, networking and publications.

A few months before the military government constituted the National Commission
on the Status of Women (NCSW), the Aurat Foundation and Shirkat Gah were planning
a large-scale consultative process towards advocacy on the issue in order to boost the
process. When the state pre-empted the plan, the Aurat Foundation and Shirkat Gah
made the strategic decision to nonetheless initiate a post-facto consultative process
involving all stakeholders, government, Commission members, civil society and
experts. This was not only to develop a common understanding on the kind of
structure, mandate and powers necessary for an effective commission, but also to
reinforce the idea that critical decisions of this nature should involve all stakeholders.
However, the major challenge was that the government as a whole was not in favour
of a strong and independent commission that would perform a watchdog role
regarding the government's own performance. Moreover the Commission members
saw the criticism of the selection process as a personal attack, and were not keen on
dialogue with rights organizations.
The objectives of the project were to:
   Work towards enabling circumstances within civil society and the government for
   the ownership, legitimacy and enhancement of the role of the NCSW to make it
   more accountable and effective in the context of women's empowerment.
   Undertake an informed consultative process between different actors, and translate
   the outcome into concrete recommendations towards strengthening the NCSW.
   Enhance understanding among policymakers and women's rights activists about the
   structure, role, powers and functioning of such state machinery as the NCSW.

The strategies used by the two women's organizations included experience sharing
with representatives of some similar commissions in other countries, a consultative
process at provincial and national levels, and lobbying for law reform. The process of
the project explores the challenges of constituting a national machinery which is
responsive to the constituency of women and yet has enough political authority to

engendering institutions

hold the entire state hierarchy accountable for advancing the gender equity agenda. Some of the dimensions explored by the project are examined below.

Engendering the process of constituting the national machinery for women (NMW) through 'constructed space'

When the military government announced its intention of setting up a permanent commission on women on 8 March 2000, some key government officials were contacted to ascertain how far the proceedings had moved and to urge them to carry out a broader consultative process. Despite this, the NCSW was created in Pakistan without any involvement of or consultation with women's organizations or civil society representatives. As such, there was no access to the decision making process through 'invited space'. In this situation, the CSO concerned with women's rights started a process to reinforce the idea that critical decisions of this nature should be made in a transparent manner in meaningful consultation with concerned stakeholders. In other words, they 'constructed space' for intervention in the policy arena. This was a 'standard-setting' procedure towards transparency and democratic process that the NCSW itself began to follow after this process.

Through a series of very strategic moves, Shirkat Gah and the Aurat Foundation were able to involve both state and civil society actors in a participatory process of sharing, reflection and consultation that had been missing in the actual creation of the NCSW. As Kabeer and Subrahmanian (1999) point out, there is a 'strong possibility of personal subjective bias entering the process of designing the goals of interventions, especially when a male-dominated institution is evolving interventions to address issues that explicitly concern women.' In this project, Shirkat Gah and the Aurat Foundation carried out 'the 'reality checks' to ensure that (the institution's) preconceptions and prejudices do not bias the design of their interventions' (Kabeer and Subrahmanian 1999).

The process started with the International Conference on National Commissions on Women in July 2001, in Islamabad, which was attended by representatives of the national commissions for women from four carefully chosen countries, India, South Africa, Philippines and United Kingdom, members of the Pakistan NCSW as well as CSO representatives. It was deliberately non-confrontational, since all conclusions emerged out of collective discussions that were based on the presentations of the international participants.

This was followed by a process to get opinions on the NCSW from the four provinces. Provincial consultations were held in North-West Frontier Province, Punjab, Sindh and Balochistan. These were attended by state officials, elected local councillors, NCSW members of that province and civil society representatives. Here the Commission members themselves were provided a space and a platform to voice their own concerns and suggestions regarding the Commission. This strategy of inclusion enabled the Commission members to 'buy in' to the recommendations emerging from the consultations. These recommendations were then compiled in the National Consultation on the NCSW, attended by existing NCSW members, participants of the earlier consultations and government department officials. The discussions focused on finalizing consensus recommendations regarding the NCSW based on the participatory consensus building process.

Engendering the national machinery itself to make it more responsive to women

Although the NCSW of Pakistan was intended to be the national machinery on women as distinct from an already existing Ministry of Women's Development, the constitution of the NCSW had left much to be desired. Its members included the chairperson of the Council of Islamic Ideology, a provincial politician, another person who held a government position and four other ex-officio members. The division of roles between the NCSW and the Ministry of Women's Development remained unclear. The mandate, autonomy and enforcing authority of the NCSW were extremely doubtful.

In this difficult situation, the Pakistan organizations' efforts to engender the NCSW show up interesting parallels to Gay Seidman's analysis of the way South African feminists were able to build gender interests into the structure of democratic institutions. Seidman (1999) brings out a sequence of processes that effectively change politics and the definition of women's interests, beginning with gender analysis, the building up of women's organizations, the articulation of a consensus agenda, the demands for legitimizing women's interests and the success of the various formal mechanisms created in response. Shirkat Gah and the Aurat Foundation built up a constituency that included not only CSOs but also government officials and, most remarkably, the members of the NCSW themselves. Through the painstaking consultative process, they achieved the articulation of a collective critique of the present constitution of the NCSW and a clear set of recommendations. The consultations focused on major areas of concern such as:
   the independence of the commission;
   role for the NCSW *vis-à-vis* the existing Ministry of Women's Development and the
   Women Development departments;
   criteria and selection process of members;
   ensuring state responsiveness (departmental cooperation, parliamentary action,
   policy advisory role);
   its powers, mandate and functions (including complaint cell);
   funding;
   rules of business;
   interaction with civil society; and
   its own accountability.

In the process of collective reflection on these issues, the members of the NCSW became aware of the gendered discourse around the issue of the national machinery for women. They not only convened a separate meeting to interact exclusively with the international participants of the first conference (who were themselves experienced members of Commissions for Women in other countries) but also had a two-day reflection exercise on the independence, mandate and membership of their own Commission. This increasing ownership of the discourse led to 'articulation of demands' by the NCSW members themselves, instead of the CSOs. The NCSW recommended changes in their own constitution through their annual report to the government. It can also be assumed that the NCSW would increase its respect for CSOs after experiencing their facilitation of such an intense learning process. They certainly became more conscious of the role the CSOs expected them to perform.

Another important dimension of the engendering process carried out by Shirkat Gah and the Aurat Foundation was that the provincial consultations enabled the NCSW members to directly interact with their primary constituency, CSOs and women's organizations, under very different circumstances from their own earlier provincial meetings. The relative absence of hierarchy provided the space for listening to each other and at least beginning to understand each other's concerns. The NCSW developed a level of responsiveness to issues and demands of CSOs. They took up sensitive issues, increased spaces for civil society participation on review committees, started addressing and intervening in prominent cases of violence against women, and protested attacks on human rights activists.

Engendering the state through a functioning NCSW by strengthening its effectiveness

The recommendations developed through the consultative process were taken up by the NCSW members themselves in their Annual Report. The government also took some responsive action, and this can be seen as a small move towards engendering the state institutions through a more effective NCSW. It is significant that the NCSW adopted the conclusions of the consultations as its own recommendations to the government, such as:
- 'It should be made incumbent on the government to place NCSW reports and recommendations before the Cabinet and the Parliament ... along with a memorandum explaining the action taken ... on the recommendations and the reasons for non-acceptance if any.'
- 'The status of the Chairperson should be that of a cabinet Minister ... with a (full-time) tenure of five years.'
- 'The NCSW mandate should include the purview of amendments to the Constitution and Pakistan's compliance with international commitments. The NCSW should be consulted on all law-making and policy formulation at the drafting stage, and should review and advise on government budgets from a gender perspective.'
- 'It should have quasi-judicial powers for purposes of investigation and to ensure compliance ... and develop mechanisms to facilitate the referral/redressal of individual grievances in any court of law.'

These recommendations serve to highlight the crucial elements of accountability and enforceability which are imperative for effectively making governments implement gender equity agenda. Further they indicate that unless the NCSW has real powers backed by political will at the highest level, it cannot truly engender the functioning of the state.

Engaging with state institutions to ensure greater roles for civil society and increasing 'voice'

The CSOs of Pakistan were wary of the military government and unwilling to be co-opted into advisory roles in the absence of democracy. However, with the initiative taken by Shirkat Gah and the Aurat Foundation, the CSOs actually began to engage with the state regarding the functioning of the NCSW. The international conference provided both CSOs and the Commission members to clarify their conjectures about the shortcomings in the constitution of the NCSW, without an open confrontation among themselves. They were also able to build joint ownership of the emergent learning and suggestions regarding effective national machineries that came from the international participants. The provincial consultations that followed the international conference were an effective medium for building up ownership among state and non-state actors such as concerned government representatives, Commission members themselves, newly elected councillors of the provinces, members of non-governmental organizations (NGOs) and capacity building organizations (CBOs), other civil society representatives and concerned individuals. It also provided women's organizations a first opportunity to reflect upon the role and composition of government machinery to mainstream women's interests. The addition of international experiences led to a deeper understanding of the entire concept of a national machinery for mainstreaming gender issues among all participants.

For several NGOs and CBOs, it was an excellent opportunity to learn about the NCSW and its mandate, when the NCSW members explained their role to these future 'clients' with whom they would have to work to fulfil their mandate. They were, in turn, able to express their expectations from the NCSW directly to the members. They were also requested to continue providing feedback[3] from the grass-roots as a mark of their ownership of the NCSW which helped to establish the crucial response-linkage to civil society which is the basis of an effective public institution of accountability. This creation of the space to express 'voice', as in 'creating a point of access to the state for groups of citizens who ... act upon shared interests'[4] enhances women's political effectiveness since it facilitates the representation of their diverse interests. As Goetz (2002) says, 'the creation of institutions to make holders of state ... power more directly accountable to women may foster more effective engagement with the state by women.'

The rich debate from these consultations brought to the surface some of the complexities surrounding the structure of a body that draws its strength and part of its mandate from women and CSOs, yet must be strongly embedded in the political realm to perform comprehensive oversight functions for the state.

Impact of these interventions

The women's organizations of Pakistan had to make a proactive effort to intervene in and engender the state decision making process which had not engaged with them of its own accord, and which had resulted in policies that bypassed the urgent concerns of women. In the process, they also mobilized the constituency of CSOs to reclaim the space to articulate their priorities. As such, their case study demonstrates that even with an apparently 'engendered institution' set up by the state, civil society needs to constantly monitor and engage with it so as to ensure that women's concerns are effectively being addressed.

The consultative process served to explore the myriad functions (redressal/referral, oversight, policy advisory, planning and monitoring) that a national machinery like the NCSW could perform, but which have to be specified for optimum effectiveness. The discussions at the international conference clarified that there could be two different roles that are played by national machineries, one when they are the only state body committed to women's agenda, and the other when they are independent watchdog bodies. A clear analysis of the Pakistan NCSW emerged using this framework.

The unique impact of this strategy of engagement, dialogue and collective capacity building was that the NCSW members took ownership of the process and its outcomes in a number of ways. They had a separate meeting with the members of the foreign commissions to strengthen their own understanding. They also mentioned the International Conference on National Commissions on Women and the regional consultations in their own Annual Report as 'a consultative process that provided (them) with considerable insight and opportunities for interaction and dialogue, ... as well as valuable information.' In the Annual Report, they also mentioned that they were trying to streamline procedures, and gave a list of recommendations for amending the Ordinance that created the NCSW. Their recommendations are almost identical to those developed during the consultative process. It was also clear that the Commission members were now in favour of consultative processes and wished to build up support from outside the NCSW. While the NCSW began to open up spaces for civil society to provide inputs, they also became more responsive to issues raised by civil society. They began taking up prominent cases of injustice and violence against women and issuing statements, as well as sensitive issues of religious ordinances.

As such, despite being a post facto process the consultations served to generate concern, ownership and renewed debate on the creation of the NCSW. It demonstrated that 'it is never too late to start a dialogue' around the gender equity agenda, especially with the state, since: 'The state, as the general regulator of society and the market, can challenge as unjust the rules that undermine the rights of relatively powerless parties ... – hence its importance for gender equity projects ... because gender-equity goals ... arouse considerable social resistance. ... (from) powerful social actors ... (maybe from) every single household' (Goetz 2002).

Notes

1 Cited in Ashworth, 1994:5, quoted in E. bell et al., BRIDGE Report no. 66, February 2002.

2 UN, 1995. URL: http://www.un.org/womenwatch/daw/beijing/platform/institu.htm.

3 Consultations in Punjab, Balochistan and Sindh provinces.

4 Moore and Joshi, 2000, quoted in Women's political effectiveness: a conceptual framework by Anne Marie Goetz, unpublished draft, 2002, p. 4.

References

Goetz, Anne Marie, 'Women's political effectiveness: a conceptual framework'. 2002. Unpublished draft.

Kabeer, Naila and Ramya Subrahmanian, 'From concepts to practice: gender aware planning through the institutional framework'. In: Naila Kabeer and Ramya Subrahmanian (eds), *Institutions, relations and outcomes: framework and case studies for gender aware planning*. London, Zed, 2000.

Seidman, Gay W., 'Gendered citizenship'. *Gender and Society*, vol. 13, no. 3 (1999), pp. 287-307.

Catherine Albertyn and Likhapha Mbatha

Customary law reform in the new South Africa

When South Africa achieved democracy in 1994, the new rights-based Constitution provided significant opportunities for reforming laws that discriminated against women. One of these was the customary law of marriage. However, reforming a system of customary law that enshrined both 'internal' and 'external' inequalities was also to constitute a challenge to the new democracy and its ability to reconcile its cultural heritage with its commitment to gender equality.

Customary law is a set of rules and practices governing the relationships and lives of black South Africans. Before 1994, it had been attributed an inferior status within the legal system of the country, reflecting a cultural imperialism that denigrated African cultures. For example, customary marriage, termed a customary union, was regarded as 'against good morals' because it was 'potentially polygynous' and was thus not legally recognized.

At the same time, customary law had become a major determinant of women's unequal status and unequal access to resources. Women married under customary law were legal minors, unable to deal in marital property, ineligible for rights to communally held land and disqualified from inheriting immovable property (Robinson 1995). Part of the reason for this was that the customary system had been manipulated by successive white governments, in collaboration with state supported male elders, into a system that distorted the original framework and principles. As a result, the codification of customary law in 1927 and subsequent court decisions entrenched and extended the subordination of women under customary law.

Traditional leaders raised the position of customary law in the new South Africa during the negotiations for the new constitution in 1993. Their request for customary law to be exempted from the Bill of Rights, and especially from the right to equality, questioned the relationship between cultural autonomy and democracy, and between customary practices and gender equality (Albertyn 1994; Murray and Kaganas 1994).

The Centre for Applied Legal Studies and the Rural Women's Movement

The Gender Research Project at the Centre for Applied Legal Studies (CALS), University of the Witwatersrand, was formed in 1992 and almost immediately became embroiled in the negotiations for the new Constitution. CALS was part of a network of women's organizations that mobilized to oppose the claims of traditional leaders for cultural autonomy. This sometimes bitterly fought contest was eventually resolved in favour of democracy in so far as customary law was rendered subject to the

Constitution. However the exact nature of the relationship between culture and equality was left open to the extent that the Constitution permitted both an oppositional relationship (in which equality could 'trump' culture) and a more integrated approach (in which cultural issues could be harmonized with constitutional values, including equality).

It was during this period that CALS began to work with the Rural Women's Movement (RWM), a rights-based organization of rural African women who were able to speak on behalf of poor, rural women. CALS established a working relationship with the RWM through providing information on the constitutional negotiations and obtaining its views on the issue of customary law and equality. An important aspect of this relationship was to assist the RWM in speaking for its members' interests and for those of the rural poor generally.

In 1995 the RWM identified reform to customary law of marriage as a key priority and asked CALS to conduct research and advocacy with them on this. This was the beginning of a more formal partnership with the RWM. CALS began a research project to find out more about how black South Africans marry. This research used social science methods to document the marriage practices of women subject to customary law, as well as their attitudes towards their status and recommendations for reform. The relevant findings of this research were as follows:
- Africans marry in accordance with both civil and customary law. For African women, the major incentive was to achieve the benefits of both systems, namely property rights and customary recognition.
- Women supported the idea of a customary marriage that gave them better status and access to, and control of resources, such as land. A recurring theme was that the position of women married under customary law needs to be clarified since the women seem to lose everything when marriage ends by death.
- Most women expressed dissatisfaction with the decisions of the civil courts which had jurisdiction over customary unions, claiming that these exhibited a bias towards men.
- The majority of women interviewed, including those in polygynous relationships, opposed the continuation of polygyny. They expressed an overall desire to become party to a civil marriage as it then made them 'safe' from becoming part of a polygynous union. Polygyny threatened the future of their property as the husband may share that property with another wife. However, women (mostly those older than the acceptable marriage age) said that they are often driven into polygynous unions out of fear of social stigmatization (being branded a spinster). It was emphasized that difficulties are experienced when a man enters a customary marriage with a rural woman, then moves to an urban area to marry a second time under civil law without declaring the first union. By and large, the majority of women involved in polygynous relationships expressed the wish that their children never be married under the same system as it is 'cruel'.

In sum, this research pointed to the importance of achieving equality – in rights and status – for women in marriage. But it also demonstrated that women wanted the cultural connections and social recognition offered by customary marriage. By the time the law reform process had begun, CALS research had been concluded and the research findings formed the basis of its advocacy strategies, both as CALS and in partnership with the RWM.

The process of law reform

Women's organizations identified customary law as priority issue for law reform by the new government. However in the immediate post-election period these organizations were only beginning to organize around specific issues and government was starting the difficult task of developing policies. Thus it was only in 1996 that the process of customary law reform began in the South African Law Commission (SALC), South Africa's statutory law reform body.

CALS' approach to customary law reform

CALS sought to engage the law reform process to shape a law that promoted women's equality within marriage at the same time as it respected positive cultural values. This had been what most respondents had supported during CALS' research and CALS wanted to ensure that the experiences and interests of women most affected by the law informed the law reform process. This meant finding ways of giving voice to the women who had been the respondents in our research and to CALS' partner, the Rural Women's Movement.

Underlying this method of engaging the state were a number of assumptions. Firstly, that this method could, in fact, generate a law that met the needs of women as expressed in our research. Secondly, that laws emanating from custom and culture could be transformed in a manner that promotes gender equality and harmonizes personal legal systems with constitutional values and international human rights norms. On a more general level, CALS sought to promote an inclusive and participatory method of law reform, especially in respect of the democratic participation by women, including women who were not part of any organized constituency but whose voices might be heard through its research and advocacy. This assumed that the state would conduct its law reform processes in an open manner.

Activities

CALS engaged the South African Law Commission directly through written submissions, attending meetings and oral advocacy with key role players. To ensure that the voices of women most affected by customary marriage were heard in the law reform process, CALS shared research findings with organizations working with rural women and encouraged them to enhance the voice of their constituency in the law reform process. It also used its research findings in its reform proposals and written and verbal submissions to the SALC and Parliament. Finally it prepared a written submission on behalf of the Rural Women's Movement, thus creating space for them to be consulted directly by the SALC.

To develop wider support within civil society, CALS sought to raise awareness on the issue and build support for its position through holding workshops with women's organizations and other stakeholders, and disseminating written summaries of findings and proposals through various media including the Gender Research Project newsletter. CALS advocacy strategies targeted the SALC and Parliament as well as stakeholders in civil society. It engaged the parliamentary process through written submissions to the relevant parliamentary committees, oral presentations to the portfolio committee, and lobbying of key Members of Parliament (MPs) and committee officials. CALS also briefed political party caucuses in Parliament.

Throughout this process, CALS had to make strategic choices about the form and content of the SALC proposals. These included decisions about a single or dual legal system, the nature of the matrimonial property regime, and the status of polygyny (SALC 1996; Goldblatt and Mbatha 1998).

Addressing polygyny

The issue of how to deal with polygyny caused much debate within CALS and the RWM. On the one hand, the research findings overwhelmingly rejected the practice as oppressive to women. However, questions were raised about the protection of women and children in existing polygynous marriages. Prohibition of polygyny would render these women even more vulnerable and marginal. In the CALS research, enormous concern had been expressed about the protection of property in polygynous marriages. In addition, certain events caused CALS to rethink the issue. Significant here was the General Annual Meeting of the RWM in February 1998, where members were chanting the slogan 'one man, one woman'. CALS noticed that some members sat down quietly without chanting the slogan. When asked why they did not chant the slogan, they replied that they were living in polygynous relationships and this prevented them from chanting the slogan. During discussions facilitated by CALS, the divisiveness of the slogan was raised. CALS became aware that women were not a homogeneous group and they did not condemn polygyny with one voice.

CALS initially suggested that a middle way of extending legal protection to such women and children be found, falling short of full recognition. However, this was difficult to translate into workable legal provisions. Members of the RWM, some of whom live in polygynous relationships, lobbied for 'serial division of property' on second, third and fourth marriages. According to this view, marital property should be divided among existing spouses every time a man wants to take an extra wife into marriage. This group also wanted women to be given an option to choose whether to become parties to polygyny or not. They knew that one of the reasons why women continue to live in polygynous relationship was fear of losing their home and the marital property to which they may have contributed. CALS advocated for this 'serial division of estates' to be incorporated in the new law, i.e. that a new contract regulating property be drawn up and made an order of court before a subsequent marriage. This was then included in the draft Bill of the SALC and became part of the subsequent law.

The Bill becomes law

The law reform process culminated in the Recognition of Customary Marriages Act, 120 of 1998. This law largely reflects what women's organizations fought for. It recognizes the equality of husband and wife in terms of status, decision making, property and children. Although it greatly improves women's rights to property in customary marriage, it does not make this retrospective. It requires that customary marriages be concluded 'in accordance with customary law'. The law legalizes polygyny, but required the consent of the parties to the marriage and a court order making arrangements for the division of property prior to entering a polygynous marriage.

Monitoring the law

Initially CALS thought that its work would end with the passing of the new law. However, this law was a radical change to the status quo in the sense that it introduced new principles, rules and enforcement mechanisms into the system of customary law. For example, it mandated equality between spouses in a situation that was previously unequal. This equality extended to women's status and decision making power in the family and society at large, as well as rights over children (guardianship and custody) and to property. The Act also brought the civil courts into a system that was previously regulated by customary courts, traditional leaders and families. It did this through requiring divorce in a civil court and, significantly, by introducing civil courts into the system of polygyny.

In supporting these provisions during the reform process, CALS had assumed that they were workable provisions and that an Act, that in theory reflected the needs of women, could do so in practice. In other words, it assumed that the gains made in the letter of the law were *sustainable* in the practice of the law. For CALS purposes, a law would be sustainable if it was fully implemented and it improved the quality of life of parties to customary marriages, especially women. This involved, firstly, scanning the legal provisions to assess whether the law, in its final form, reflected women's interests. Secondly, it meant working to ensure that the law was fully implemented and, thirdly, it entailed measuring whether the law changes women's quality of life, especially with regard to their ability to access and own property during and after marriage. Of course, these steps were all inter-related.

As these issues emerged, CALS decided that it needed to continue with the project on the customary law of marriage to influence and monitor the implementation of the Act. In deciding to do this, CALS recognized that a concern with women's rights cannot stop at the point of advocating for law reform, but should go on to engage with the process of implementing the law and evaluating whether the practice of the law meets the intentions of the advocates for the law.

Assessing the legal provisions

In the preliminary scan of legal provisions, at least one problem emerged. The provisions requiring consent of parties to a customary marriage do not make specific provision for polygynous marriages. Hence they speak about consent of two parties only. This is clearly a problem in that it does not achieve the goal of requiring consent of a previous wife or wives, as well as a prospective wife. It needs to be amended through in Parliament.

Problems of implementation

It was clear at an early stage that there were several obstacles to achieving a sustainable law through the effective implementation of the Act. Indeed, the report of the Parliamentary Committee at the time the law was passed had identified the twin problems of financial resources and state capacity. It is perhaps not surprising, therefore, that there was a two-year delay in implementing the Act which only became effective in November 2000.

During this period, CALS engaged the Department of Justice about the content of the Regulations that were being prepared to guide the application of the law. Here CALS was particularly concerned that the Regulations comply with the progressive content of the law. It also disseminated information to NGOs about progress on the Regulations and lobbied the Department to promulgate the law.

The Act seeks to protect customary practices that are compatible with the Constitution. The assumption underlying this was that these practices still resonated within communities. It was also assumed that the Act was capable of accommodating both the variety of customary practices, as well as changes in these practices. If it was not able to do this, then further reform of the Act would be necessary. CALS was anxious to shape the interpretation of the law to ensure this end and sought to pre-empt problems of interpretation and application by the Courts by lobbying for training of magistrates and volunteering to write a Bench Book for magistrates to refer to in applying the Act. CALS also identified the need to engage in test case litigation to clarify interpretations of the Act.

Monitoring

CALS' key objective in monitoring the law was to assess it from the perspective of those whom it believed should benefit from the law. It was the experiences of these women that it sought in understanding any problems with implementation. It was also the experiences of these women that it used to guide proposed solutions to these problems.

Identifying the standards
CALS sought to measure the law against the purpose of the various provisions as influenced by women and as determined in the law reform process. These became the initial standards against which to measure progress.

An initial list of issues
CALS then identified kinds of problems of implementation that had already emerged or could influence the ability of the Act to improve women's lives. These included:
- Problems of state capacity: the Act requires registering officers to register all customary marriages. The Department of Home Affairs, responsible for such registration, initially indicated that it did not have sufficient capacity to provide these officers or the other facilities required to undertake such registration.
- Problems of the capacity of courts: the Act requires that High Courts and Divorce Courts adjudicate over disputes arising from customary marriages. This raises

problems of access as there are less than twenty of these Courts for the entire
country and most are situated in the urban centres. In addition, because customary
law is being brought into the official courts, all of the wider problems related to
transforming of the Justice System come into play here. These include the lack of
resources to provide adequate court facilities, trained staff and social context
exposure.
- Problems of legal literacy: the majority of people to whom this Act applies are poor,
  uneducated and have little access to information about the new law and how to use
  it. Since the Act improves the position of women, it is women who are most likely to
  want to make use of it. But it is rural women who are the most impoverished and
  disempowered in South Africa.
- Problems of gendered attitudes within society: social and cultural norms that view
  women as minors still persist amongst women and men in many communities. In
  many cases, women have internalized ideas of their own inferior status. These
  constitute barriers to the Act and its recognition of women's equality. They are also
  exacerbated by women's financial dependence on men.
- Problems of resistance from traditional leaders: resistance from some traditional
  leaders, especially around the provisions equalizing women's status in customary
  marriage suggested that women may encounter resistance within communities
  when attempting to register their customary marriages using the new law. This may
  mean that despite the positive reforms in the new Act, many women will remain
  unprotected by the law and the Constitution.

Collecting data
CALS then conducted preliminary research on the Act by collecting information on
whether and how the Act had impacted on the lives of women connected to the
original research sites. These women were more likely to have knowledge of the Act
as they lived in or near communities who had been consulted during its development.
The initial research findings thus related largely to problems within the state rather
within communities. We discuss one set of findings relating to registration. Here
problems of state capacity and of gendered attitudes of officials were apparent.

Registration of customary marriage
The Act allows one or both spouse/s to apply for a customary marriage to be
registered. This includes marriages in existence before the commencement of the
Act. Third parties can also initiate registration by alerting a marriage officer to the
existence of a customary marriage. These provisions arose partly from the CALS
research that demonstrated that men are reluctant to register their marriages. They
therefore attempt to circumvent problems women have had in getting men to register
their marriages.

The monitoring research sought to establish how registration worked in practice and
to document any problems experienced by community members and registering
officers. The main problems identified related to the question of access because of:
- too few or insufficiently trained officials;
- lack of knowledge of registration requirements by users; or
- practices of officials arising out of lack of knowledge of, misinterpretation of, or
  problems with registration requirements. In particular, officials generally refused

to register marriages at the instance of only one party, even where there was objective evidence of the marriage.

As CALS identified problems, it sought to address them through engaging the relevant government officials around solutions. These solutions included expanding the number of officials, improved training for existing officials and advising communities about available registering officers. In addition, CALS sought to persuade Home Affairs staff to adopt a more nuanced approach to registration requirements, to accept objective evidence and to explain the reasons for refusing registration to persons requesting it.

However, the fact that officials tended to refuse to register marriages at the request of women, and sent them home to fetch their husbands, remains a serious impediment to the intention of providing women with accessible registration in the face of recalcitrant husbands. There is ample evidence to show that men are reluctant to register their customary marriages. However, officials do not use the information submitted to them by women to register marriages. This requires further engagement with the state to remedy the situation. At present, the Act is not meeting the needs of women and the intention of the drafters.

Ongoing monitoring research and advocacy
In general, CALS is involved on ongoing research and advocacy around the implementation of the Act and its ability to improve the quality of women's lives. It continues to assess whether the new law addresses the problems identified by women in respect of the old law. These include:
- problems of minority legal status and access to property during marriage;
- lack of decision making power; and
- non-consensual polygyny.

In many instances, it is too early to evaluate the impact of the Act and this research is still ongoing. In addition, some of the problems experienced by women relate to issues of access to property upon the death of their spouse. These have been taken up by CALS within other law reform processes, especially the reform of the customary law of succession.

Engaging attitudes
CALS has only begun to skim the surface of the problem of attitudes. Its approach to customary law reform has been to advocate for the retention of positive customary values and practices, and their harmonization with constitutional values. Its strategies have been to engage communities and stakeholders, such as traditional leaders, in a discourse that pays attention to culture and to the need for gender equality. However, it has proved to be very difficult to mediate the language of culture and the language of rights, and it is easy for discussion to polarize rights against culture. Part of the reason for this is that the concepts differ. Customary law emphasizes obligations, while constitutional discourse emphasizes rights. In addition, there is little, if any, public discourse in South Africa that seeks to contest conservative or patriarchal cultural claims in a progressive manner. CALS managed to give women living under customary law a voice in the law reform process. It

remains a challenge to do so in the implementation of the law – a task that ultimately requires a more widespread engagement of gendered cultural norms and values in our society.

Lessons

Engendered law reform requires a positive context. Firstly, the context of a democratic constitution with a commitment to gender equality and to open and participatory governance created a positive political climate for engendered law reform in South Africa. However, it was only when the state was open to reform that civil society was able to make an impact. This occurred when the state demonstrated a willingness and a *capacity* to engage the issues in detail, beyond a rhetorical commitment to gender equality.

Once the process started within the state, civil society participation was made possible by the open procedures of the SALC and Parliament. However, the knowledge that CALS had acquired (through its research) made it a very useful resource for the state institutions. Hence, CALS strategy of engaging in research was a highly successful one that gave it the tools and authority to engage the state in the law reform process.

CALS learned that law making is an imperfect process and that strategic choices and compromises have to be made along the way. It sought to make these with reference to women's experience and needs as evident in research and consultations.

CALS assumed that knowledge of women's lives was critical to influencing law reform that will ultimately benefit women. In the law reform process, this knowledge was important to CALS' ability to formulate positions, engage in advocacy and serve our constituency of rural women. However, one cannot tell from the law reform process itself whether that assumption was true. It is only through the ongoing monitoring process that one can learn whether the law, in fact, benefits women.

CALS was concerned to give women a voice in the law reform process. Its method of participatory research provided an important basis for doing this and helped to bridge the gap between experts/academics and community-based women.

An effective partnership means that one must create legitimacy, establish a mandate and include political and technical strengths. CALS established its legitimacy by working closely with the RWM and by empowering its members to lobby government for law reform. CALS also broadened its support base from women's organizations through workshops on their research. Through this process, CALS profiled itself as an expert which allowed for strategic interventions and advocacy in the parliamentary process, playing a critical role in linking the content of the bill to the needs and experiences of women, and reflecting customary practices.

The monitoring research required CALS to engage the state constantly. It had to develop relationships with key officials and open the channels of communication in order to influence the implementation of the law. This process was assisted by a climate of openness in the state and the willingness of officials to interact.

Through the process of monitoring, CALS learned that while many problems lie in the state, attitudes within society constitute a barrier of unknown magnitude. A key lesson was therefore that it should perhaps have done more during the law reform process to engage attitudes and to contribute to a more conducive environment for women to exercize their legal rights. The women's movement has traditionally engaged the state in South Africa over the past decade. While it needs to continue to do this, it also needs to expand its activities to engage civil society role players in attitudes about women. CALS' research highlights the critical need for women's movements to work more in this area. It also highlights the need to engage in the difficult task of developing voices that are able to speak within and across cultural and constitutional discourses.

References

Albertyn, C., 'Women and the transition to democracy'. *Acta Juridica*, 1994.

Goldblatt, B. and L. Mbatha, 'Gender, culture and equality: reforming customary law'. In: C. Albertyn (ed.), *Engendering the political agenda: a South African case study*. Centre for Applied Legal Studies, University of Witwatersrand, 1998. A shorter version has appeared as Chapter 3 in 'Engendering the political agenda: the role of the state, women's organisations and the international community. Santo Domingo, INSTRAW, 2000.

'The harmonisation of the common law and indigenous law'. *Issue Paper Customary Marriages*. Project 90. Pretoria, South African Law Commission (SALC), August 1996.

Murray, C. and F. Kaganas, 'The contest between culture and gender equality under South Africa's interim constitution'. *Journal of Law and Society*, vol. 21, no. 409 (1994).

Robinson, K., 'The minority and subordinate status of African women under customary law'. *South African Journal on Human Rights*, vol. 11, no. 457 (1995).

Liz Frank and Elizabeth Khaxas

A case study of the 50/50 campaign in Namibia, focusing on women's grass-roots participation

Sister Namibia was founded in 1989 on the eve of Namibia's independence in 1990. The organization is a feminist non-governmental women's organization that aims to give women a voice in the building of a democratic post-colonial society. We work to raise awareness among all people of the ways in which political, social, cultural, legal and economic systems of power control and oppress girls and women. We advocate for democratic change through promoting the full protection of the human rights of all girls and women, and opposing and challenging sexism, racism, homophobia and other discourses and practices that divide people. We engage in the fields of media, education, training, research, advocacy and cultural activities in order to promote women's full participation in bringing about a world free from violence, discrimination and oppression.

In 1998, Sister Namibia conducted research on women's participation in politics and decision making in Namibia.[1] We disseminated our findings in March 1999 at a workshop attended by women in non-governmental organizations (NGOs), political parties and elected women at all levels of government, and used this meeting to collectively strategize ways of increasing women's participation in the political process. At this workshop, Sister Namibia was mandated to lead the NGOs, women's wings of political parties and other organizations during our preparations for the December 1999 National Assembly elections to promote the democratic participation of women in the elections and beyond. A major decision taken at that workshop was to call for 50% women candidates on 'zebra-style' party lists (alternating women and men candidates on the lists) for the 1999 elections, and to spell out women's concerns in a Namibian Women's Manifesto. Thus was born the 50/50 Campaign.

Background

The Constitution of the Republic of Namibia, adopted in 1990, includes a Bill of Rights that gives

> *(all) citizens ...the right to participate in peaceful political activity intended to influence the composition and policies of the government, the right to participate in the conduct of public affairs, whether directly or through freely chosen representatives, and to form and join political parties, to vote and be eligible for election (Article 1[2]).*

Given the history of oppression through colonial and apartheid rule, the restoration of human dignity and the achievement of true equality are fundamental values underlying the Constitution. The Constitution recognizes that some groups within

Namibia suffered special discrimination because of their sex or race as a result of past laws and practices, and allows for Parliament to pass affirmative action laws aimed at redressing such discrimination. Article 23 states that

> ... it shall be permissible to have regard to the fact that women in Namibia have traditionally suffered special discrimination and that they need to be encouraged to play a full, equal and effective role in the political, social, economic and cultural life of the nation.

On the basis of the above, Parliament adopted affirmative action provisions for the local authority elections held in 1992, which contributed to the fact that 37% of elected local councillors were women. The affirmative action measures were strengthened in 1998, as a result of which women's numerical representation increased to 41%. Through by-elections more women have come into office, such that Namibia currently has 43% women at the local authority level, and 40% of the mayors are women. The current President of the Association of Local Authorities in Namibia is a woman who has stepped into the footsteps of two women presidents before her.

The local authority elections of 1992 and 1998 were conducted using the party list system, while the Local Authorities Act stipulated that future elections at the local level would be conducted on a constituency-based system, making no reference to affirmative action provisions in this system. Over the past three years, the women's movement lobbied government and political parties to retain the party list system, fearing that with the new system, women's numerical representation of over 40% at the local level would drop drastically to the 4% women that we currently have at the regional level, where elections take place in constituencies. In November 2002, the Local Authorities Act was amended to retain the party list system, with a number of Members of Parliament (MPs) referring to the benefits for women in their motivation for the amendment.

At the national level, 29% of parliamentarians currently in the National Assembly are women, elected through party lists, while 71% are men. In the National Council, which has two representatives elected from each of Namibia's 13 Regional Councils, only two (8%) of the 26 members are women, while 92% are men, reflecting the small percentage of women elected at the regional level. Yet women constitute 51% of the population and 52% of the electorate in Namibia.

Goals and strategies of the 50/50 Campaign, 1999-2002

The following objectives and strategies were planned for the 50/50 Campaign to promote women's equal participation in politics and decision making:
- Raising awareness on the importance of women's participation in politics and decision making among women, NGOs, political parties, state actors and the general public.
- Mobilizing women to take on the challenge of leadership within their communities in order to increase the number of women at all levels of politics and decision making.
- Providing training in advocacy and lobbying skills regarding gender, citizenship and governance.

- Lobbying Parliament, the Executive, Regional and Local Government, the Electoral Commission and political parties for the amendment of the electoral laws to install a quota system that will increase women's access to elected positions at local, regional and national level and culminating in a '50/50 Bill'.
- Promoting legal literacy among women by the collective development of specific demands for affirmative action legislation providing for women's greater or equal access to elected positions at all levels of government.
- Lobbying political parties to develop systems of selecting candidates that are fair to both women and men.

The Campaign was led by the Namibian Women's Manifesto Network (referred to as the Network in this paper), with Sister Namibia as the lead agency. The Network is a loose structure bringing together women leaders from towns and villages all over Namibia with members of national NGOs based in Windhoek to lobby for the implementation of demands contained in the Namibian Women's Manifesto. The Network grew out of the first phase of the Campaign, conducted in 1999, when we presented our research into women's political participation in Namibia. We developed and published the Manifesto in seven languages, promoting our 'gender agenda' and calling for gender balanced 'zebra-style' candidate lists for the National Assembly elections held in December 1999. We conducted a Training of Trainers workshop for women leaders from regional centres and major towns in all 13 regions of Namibia, who then facilitated local workshops to raise awareness on women's political and human rights and popularize the 50/50 demand. The response to the Manifesto was overwhelming: participants at the workshops took it as their own and began using it as a tool to voice their concerns. Through the Manifesto, thousands of women began to realise that they had rights as women, as equal human beings to men. The Namibian Women's Manifesto thus served as a much-needed tool in the long and arduous struggle of restoring women's dignity after decades of apartheid and centuries of patriarchal rule. The Namibian Women's Manifesto Network and the 50/50 Campaign developed out of this response.

In phase 2, in 2000 the Campaign focused broadly on the issue of increasing women's participation in politics and decision making. We developed a pamphlet and two posters to popularize our demand for the equal representation of women and men in elected positions of government. We called on political parties to include 50% women as candidates on 'zebra' party lists in all future elections, and lobbied Parliament to amend the electoral laws to bring about gender balance in elected positions at all three levels of government. We held two National Training of Trainers workshops for the facilitators of the Network from the regions, who then conducted their own workshops with the campaign materials in 22 towns and villages across the country.

At the national level we held meetings with leaders of political parties and parliamentary standing committees to introduce our demands. We also made sure we received a lot of media coverage for our activities. We further collected more than 2500 signatures in a short time under a petition calling for laws that put women in half of all elected positions of government. This petition was handed to the Speaker of the National Assembly after a march to Parliament conducted by the Network and many supporting NGOs. With this Campaign we became part of the global campaign

women's grass-roots participation

'50/50 by 2005: Get the Balance Right!' that was launched by NGOs in New York in June 2000, parallel to the United Nations Review of the Implementation of the Beijing Platform for Action.

During the third phase of the Campaign, between 2001-2002, we commissioned research on mechanisms used around the globe to promote women's access to elected positions of government as well as the 50/50 options for Namibia. These options were endorsed at a National Consultative Meeting for all members of the Network. This was followed by the development of the '50/50 Bill', which was launched at a second National Consultative Meeting. Local workshops and lobbying activities were organized around the country following both consultative meetings, targeting political parties and church leaders as well as regional and town and village councils, traditional leaders and community leaders. At the national level we organized public discussion events, conducted an intensive media campaign in the major local languages and arranged contact meetings with relevant Parliamentary Standing Committees. All these activities were used to lobby stakeholders on the importance of supporting the adoption by Parliament of gender balance legislation regarding elections.

The lawmakers agreed in general with our demands, although some argued that women were not ready for political office yet as they lacked education and experience. None of the thousands of women consulted at the grass-roots level were of this opinion, but it became apparent that the ruling party planned to promote the Southern African Development Community (SADC) call for 'at least 30% women by 2004' as a 'first step'. Ironically, perhaps not least through pressure from the 50/50 Campaign, we have now already achieved this target in the National Assembly, as both the ruling party and the UDF (United Democratic Front) replaced outgoing male MPs with women.

Sister Namibia conducted action research on the third phase of the 50/50 Campaign, and our findings are presented below, focusing on the impact of the Campaign on women's grass-roots participation.

Recruiting participants for broad representation and participation

Participants were recruited from towns and villages in all regions of Namibia as well as members of national NGOs based in the capital, Windhoek. The participants from towns and villages are the backbone of the Network, organizing and facilitating workshops and advocacy activities in their communities after receiving training from Sister Namibia.

The majority of facilitators we recruited are poor women from rural and marginalized urban areas, including the unemployed; subsistence farmers; domestic workers; and women living in squatter camps or small rural settlements. Some women were already members of community organizations or self-help groups. We also invited community activists, including teachers, social workers, nurses and community development officers in urban and rural areas who work with poor women or who have access to poor women in villages and towns.

We recruited poor women from diverse communities as participants for this project because women constitute the poorest of the poor in Namibia and we wanted to channel our limited resources (both material and skills) towards this group. Poor women are also the most excluded from formal political activities in Namibia because of their class and gender, yet they are also the ones who are maintaining families and holding communities together. We therefore decided that levels of literacy or formal education should not be criteria for participation. New members were not asked their party affiliation, and were requested to leave party politics aside in their work in the Network. Facilitators requested permission to bring in women they knew from neighbouring communities. Others called for the inclusion of women from ethnic or language groups that were not yet represented. Facilitators thus took ownership for building the Network in an effort to make this a truly nationwide project.

Why did we choose grass-roots women to lead the Campaign rather than lobby government directly? Thirteen years after Namibia's independence, we have a ruling party, the South West African People's Organization (SWAPO) which has a two-thirds majority in Parliament. Despite the many provisions in the Constitution promoting the rights of women, many urgent and important Bills affecting women have been held up in endless delays in Parliament. For this reason, we felt that by framing our project as an action conducted by ordinary and poor women, we would show that it is possible for poor people to develop laws and lobby for them.

We also successfully recruited new facilitators from places where we had not been active before, in an attempt to have as broad a participation as possible. For this we used phone book recruitment, recruitment through radio, and through other NGOs and networks, and contact with local leaders such as pastors, village councillors, school principals or health workers.

The women we approached in this way were often surprised to learn that members of their community had identified them as (potential) leaders, and we spent some time on the telephone motivating them to participate. This method of recruitment sometimes led to a shared responsibility for the local activities by the person who had nominated the new facilitator. One principal provided accommodation at his school for participants from other villages, the school matron helped cook the goat provided by the headman, and school children made posters advertising the workshop. The whole village rallied to make sure 'their' Network facilitator was going to make a success of it.

Our use of radio was limited to one indigenous official language. (There are 11 in Namibia.) We broadcast our calls for interested women to contact us for information. We focused on this particular language service, as the Sister Namibia staff involved in the project were fluent in this language and were able to develop good relations with the staff.

In the north, where half of Namibia's population live and most of whom are supporters of the ruling party, this method failed us. We encountered hostility towards our work which was seen as a threat to SWAPO. We therefore developed another recruitment strategy which was to go through other NGOs and networks active in those regions. In this way we were able to recruit two teachers from secondary schools, who recruited three more facilitators from other small towns or villages. However, we were aware that these five facilitators would not be able to impact much in this populous part of the country.

Town and village facilitators were the implementers of the Campaign at the local level while the members of national NGOs gave advice in the planning stages and supported activities at the national level.

Training programmes for consultation, education and advocacy at the local level

Sister Namibia designed and conducted two training workshops for the town and village facilitators of the Network to enable them to carry out consultation, education and advocacy in their local communities. Our training programme sought to enable the newly joined facilitators to understand the history, aims, content and context of the Campaign, and know how to plan, organize and conduct their own local workshop and advocacy activities as well as build their women's groups. In this section we will briefly describe some aspects of the training and analyze its effectiveness.

As our consultative meeting had been in English, we decided to begin the training workshops with a photo slide presentation in three local languages. Not all facilitator had been able to follow the English, and this time, many facilitators added their own remarks and stories, which caused much laughter, eased the tension for newcomers and gained the stalwarts recognition and affirmation for the work done so far. Illiterate women in particular commented that the slide presentation was a good way of documenting our history. Following the slide talk, the facilitators received a handout with a short history of the Network in two languages to help them prepare for their local workshops. All training was conducted in three languages.

We also held small group discussions on the current status of women's political representation in Namibia, and the many barriers preventing women from participating in politics and decision making. This led to a discussion on why women should participate and what changes they could bring to the lives of women and other marginalized groups in the community. Participants linked good governance to their everyday living, to freedom from poverty and violence, and the right to housing and education for their children.

Training on the options and demands for gender balance in elected positions of government was the core content of our project, and we used role-plays to demonstrate the provisions of the '50/50 Bill'. We also developed and printed the 50/50 Pamphlet in seven languages to explain the provisions of the Bill in simple terms.

Through the training and the pamphlet, facilitators gained legal literacy by learning to understand the electoral acts and discussing draft amendments to these acts. They realized that gender balance can easily be achieved through law reform, and through their participation in our workshops and campaign activities claimed the '50/50 Bill' as theirs. They now want to see this law passed, and many are prepared to keep the Campaign going in one form or another until this goal is achieved.

The facilitators further received training on the national laws and international agreements on which the Network has based its demand for gender balance in elected positions of government. These were also summarized in the pamphlet. They learnt to understand their citizenship rights as guaranteed in the Constitution, and how affirmative action provisions have already brought many women into local government. Many were surprised to learn that our demand is not something that we just want as women but that it is guaranteed by the laws and policies of our country and the international instruments signed by our government. As one participant commented:

> I never realised the importance of our Constitution and the National Gender Policy but now I know parts of them well. These are powerful documents that need to be implemented in the interests of women.

Our training on lobbying and advocacy focused on five main strategies, namely contact activities, the distribution of the pamphlet, a signature campaign, a local march and media work. The facilitators understood that we would use these strategies to build visibility and support for our campaign. They learnt about their constitutional citizenship rights to freedom of information and expression, freedom of assembly and peaceful demonstration as means of participation in decision making. We stressed that the facilitators should involve their women's groups and other women of their towns and villages in organizing and conducting all the activities of the Campaign, and use the Campaign to build the local women's movement.

Another major component of our training was to discuss the importance of collaboration across the many differences among women, such as language, ethnicity, education, class, political affiliation, (dis)ability and sexual orientation. The facilitators could see for themselves that this was not rhetoric but something that we practised as Sister Namibia, by recruiting women leaders regardless of who they were and by being open about our diversities and constructing them as strengths rather than as liabilities. As one participant said: 'We may seem to be so different yet we share so much oppression as women.'

At the end of both training workshops, each facilitator received a file with the contents of the workshop prepared in two languages to assist them with conducting their local workshops and lobbying activities. The files further provided logistical support by including an invitation letter to the local workshop explaining the aims and objectives of the workshop and the 50/50 Campaign; a programme and a registration form for the local workshop; a comprehensive report schedule to give feedback on all the local activities; and information on the responsibilities of town and village facilitators in terms of their preparations and facilitation of the workshop and local lobbying activities, as well as their accountability for money matters.

As part of the first national training workshop in Windhoek, the facilitators visited Parliament to learn how it operates and how it can be accessed by citizens. An attempt at meeting with members of the Parliamentary Women's Caucus during the second National Training Workshop failed, despite being requested long in advance, as we were informed too late to reschedule the visit that Parliament was sitting at that time. However, overall the visits had a strong impact by demystifying this institution and giving poor women and rural women an initial contact to lawmakers who are there on their behalf and accountable to them. Several participants reported that these visits had helped them to overcome barriers in approaching local state actors to request support for the Campaign.

Our main challenges with regard to the training were the short time available to cover the context and content of the Campaign as well as the different lobbying and advocacy strategies through which the Campaign would be implemented. Working with women who were at different levels of education and understanding was also challenging, as we had to make training meaningful for different groups of participants. Working in three different languages was also time-consuming and stressful for those trainers who could speak these languages.

As a result of Sister Namibia's training for Network facilitators, the following activities took place at the local level: some 105 workshops were held (in two or three rounds) in 55 towns and villages, at which the Network facilitators were able to directly involve 3500 people, mainly women but also a number of men. The participants enthusiastically supported our demands for amendments to the electoral laws to ensure gender balance at all three levels of government in all future elections. Through their contact activities at the local level, the facilitators and their committees or groups brought the message of gender balance in government to 70 schools, 88 churches, nine traditional leaders, 17 regional councillors and 32 local councillors. They held meetings with NGOs and leaders of all major political parties, and many were able to solicit the public support of government leaders including local and regional councillors, mayors and regional governors. They distributed thousands of pamphlets, collected hundreds of signatures and held marches to local authorities to hand over the signatures and the '50/50 Bill'. A number of them were able to access the media to publicize and report, and to mobilize participation and support for their local events.

The impact of consultation, education and advocacy at the local level

In this section we will analyze the impact of the consultation, education and advocacy activities conducted by the Network facilitators in their communities. While responses by women were positive in all the regions, there was a stark contrast between the largely positive responses of church leaders and school staff, local and regional state actors, political parties and traditional leaders in most parts of the country compared to community leaders in the north.

Mobilizing women

All the facilitators of the Network reported great interest and participation by women in their communities in the local workshops and lobbying activities, and strong support among the participants for the demands of our campaign. Interest ran particularly high in small communities, where not many workshops take place. One facilitator described the women as 'being hungry for training.' Another said, 'Women in our town first thought that participation in politics was only for men and not for women. Now that they have seen that they can participate in any political activity,

gender, citizenship and governance

...hey believe that they can become councillors and governors.' There was a strong emphasis by participants of the local workshops on solidarity and women supporting each other, asserting that 'women should support each other in elections and should unite in solidarity, so that party politics should not divide them.' Women also agreed that poor and uneducated women could be leaders. Further, women gained a new understanding of responsible and passionate citizenship and their right to use the tools of building democracy: 'Many women did not understand that it is our right to march... (that) we are teaching people democracy.'

Support from men

The facilitators reported a broad range of reactions to the 50/50 Campaign from men. The two extremes were expressed as follows: 'Some men came to my office and said that I am instigating their wives, and some women did not come because their men were against it.' ...'There was one man from Okaukuejo who stayed for the whole workshop. At the end he said that he would inform the women at Okaukuejo about what he learnt, particularly the San women there.'
A number of men supported the local workshops by taking minutes, cooking food and encouraging their family members to participate, although leaving men behind became a major area of concern for some of the participants at the first round of workshops and it was reported that 'most participants wanted their husbands to be here' because they are the ones that have to change in terms of sharing power. Facilitators therefore later started to invite men, but they stressed that much more needs to be done in the future to involve men in the activities of the Network.

Support from churches

Many facilitators reported strong support from churches in their communities. In one case, '...the pastor and the church board... wished me all the strength for the work that we are doing.' Where church leaders were not supportive, they were put under pressure. One woman reported telling an unsupportive church elder that 'when the church board is elected, women have to be half of it. I also gave him the pamphlet to distribute at his church.' This strong support from the churches was partly due to our involvement of church leaders in the recruitment of local facilitators for the Campaign, which gave them a responsibility to support the women they had identified. Also, churches are places where communities share information about local events, and many facilitators made use of this public space to announce their local workshops and other activities to their congregation. Further, women represent the majority of churchgoers while men dominate the church leadership. This placed male pastors under pressure to do something in support of women. While our demand for gender balance in leadership was directed towards the state and not towards the church itself, in some cases church leaders themselves made this link and expressed the need for church reform in this regard.

Support from schools

Many facilitators were invited by teachers or school principals to speak to children at their schools about gender issues in general, and some facilitators who are teachers themselves were able to bring the Campaign into their own schools: 'I told (my principal and the students) that women should get to know their rights on school boards and in other organisations.' As with the pastors, our success was partly due to school principals having identified facilitators in their communities. Some facilitator also approached women teachers to assist them with the planning and organizing of their workshops. School halls were utilized for the workshops and other meetings. In some cases school principals agreed to give the keynote address at the workshops, which influenced teachers to attend the workshops and support the advocacy and lobbying activities.

Support from local and regional state actors

In most places, the Network facilitators received strong support from local and regional councillors and other state actors. Some reported as follows: 'I spoke to the Mayor, and the councillors from DTA, CoD[3] and SWAPO. All these councillors were positive.' The Regional Governor of Erongo Region 'told the women to unite and vote for female candidates in the next election and not male candidates'[4] when he received the '50/50 Bill'.

However, not all regional and local councillors were in full support: 'One councillor said that the '50/50 Bill' should have been drawn up by the Ministry of Women Affairs and not by NGOs.' Some male councillors confronted facilitators with outright sexism: 'I was shocked to hear how the people we have elected spoke about women. They said things like "women should first get educated, women are stupid, why should we elect them, they must get training." ' On encountering a councillor who had not appeared at a workshop, one woman recounted how she challenged him:

> The councillor did not attend our workshop even while he was invited. When I met with him again in the street I asked him why he did not attend and he said he forgo I told him that he must just remember one thing, that in December the women will march to his office and he should not say that he did not know anything about this issue. 'This was the second time we have been inviting you to our workshop and you are not coming.'

The strong impact of our lobbying and advocacy at the local and regional level was reflected by the outcomes of a strategic planning meeting of the Namibian Elected Women's Forum held in July 2002, which brought together women in local and regional government with women MPs across party lines to strategise how to increas women's participation in politics. The Elected Women's Forum drafted a vision statement stating:

> We, the elected women will fight for a 50% representation of women at all levels of government, i.e. national, regional and local, and within parastatals, the private sector and NGOs. We will also through our coordinated and united efforts support the current representation of elected women at all levels, until an equal representation is achieved.[5]

support from political parties

Most facilitators reported that they were able to meet with representatives of political parties in their communities, and generally received support for their demands. The fact that by-elections were taking place in a number of communities at the time of our campaign led to strong support for our 50/50 demands as political parties competed for the votes of women. At the same time, the facilitators in most regions were able to challenge the divisiveness of party politics by inviting women from different political parties to their workshops and gaining their support: 'At our local workshop I informed the two women councillors present that they are there to represent all women and not their political parties.' Facilitators themselves were able to demonstrate going beyond party politics to the people of their communities: 'Being a CoD member myself, at first when I was doing the workshop people were looking at me with that eye. But from the second workshop people have seen that I was trying to do something for the community.'

support from traditional leaders

It was the facilitators from small towns and villages that had most success with reaching out to traditional leaders. As one facilitator noted: 'The headman also supported, he said that things like this were not happening in our village and he wishes us well.' An additional bonus emerged from the fact that a number of Network facilitators are traditional leaders themselves. After addressing a meeting of traditional leaders, one such participant 'told them that if they are not supporting government promises made to women, one day they might regret this. Women are standing up, women are the majority of voters, and we might even start our own party. They then said that they had to support the idea, because it is in the Constitution.'

lack of support in the north of Namibia

As mentioned before, the penetration of our campaign did not reach into the populous north of Namibia, apart from five facilitators who we managed to recruit. The north is characterized by strong political support for the majority political party, and our campaign was quickly labelled as promoting an opposition party. In addition, there have been a number of denouncements on homosexuality and lesbianism from SWAPO leaders, both men and women and including the President, and our campaign was identified as 'promoting lesbianism'.

good practices

In the following we summarize the good practices that emerged for us from this campaign. We believe that they are the ingredients for future campaigns of this nature.

research

Our Campaign was based on research, which examined international strategies to increase women's participation in politics as well as Namibian election laws, and made recommendations for the Namibian context. The research provided legitimacy to our demands and laid the foundation for all the other campaign strategies including consultation, training, lobbying and advocacy and the development of the '50/50 Bill'.

National recruitment of town and village facilitators and building of a local support base for the facilitators

In a context such as ours where there are only a handful of women's organizations, most of them based in the capital Windhoek, it was necessary to recruit other women with leadership potential in small towns and villages in order to take the Campaign to the local level. The use of institutions, such as churches and schools through which the facilitators were recruited, provided support for the facilitators at the local level.

Training of facilitators

Training the facilitators was a crucial strategy in ensuring that they were well informed on the content and strategies of the Campaign, and gained the necessary advocacy and lobbying skills. The training provided the facilitators with knowledge on gender issues broadly, issues of gender and governance in particular, and the skill to implement the Campaign at the local level.

National and local consultations to build informed participation and ownership of the Campaign

Consultations provided a platform for the different stakeholders to come together to plan, give advice and share information on strategies for increasing women's participation in politics. This is the first time in the history of Namibia that poor women were consulted on law reform both at national and local levels, and their input valued. This contributed to informed participation and built broad ownership of the Campaign.

Working with and beyond difference on a common agenda

We were able to involve women from different ethnic and language groups, regions, political parties, classes, age groups, physical abilities and sexual orientations to work on a common agenda. This was only possible because we were able to recognize and acknowledge our differences and work with those differences in order to achieve a common goal. Our Network is a sign of hope for Namibia that collaboration is possible even in a context highly stratified by ethnicism, hegemonic party politics, strong expressions of state homophobia and stark divisions brought about by class. We had to deal with all these differences and analyze them to see why and for whom they were a threat, and then to move onto the business that brought us together. We did not have to deny or 'invisibilize' aspects of identity of any one of us in order to work together.

Developing and strengthening of women leaders and women's organizations at the local level

The work of the facilitators led in many towns and villages to the forming and strengthening of women's organizations at the local level. This was made possible because the Campaign activities provided opportunities for women to identify and find solutions for local concerns. The work of the facilitators for their communities constructed them as leaders. Through their actions, the facilitators redefined leadership as something that is not determined by the level of one's wealth or education but as something that is determined by one's work and actions.

Using media to mobilize women and to raise public awareness

We made extensive use of the media to create visibility for the Campaign, thereby raising public awareness as well as mobilizing women. This was made possible because of the good contacts and relationships the Campaign organizers and facilitators built with the media. Long after the Campaign has ended, the media is continuing to raise the issue of women's participation and bring coverage of what is happening in other countries around this issue, and the term '50/50' had become part of mainstream discourse.

Evaluation and monitoring of the Campaign activities

We conducted two in-depth collaborative monitoring and evaluation exercises, one in the middle and one almost at the end of the Campaign. These were based on comprehensive reporting formats provided in advance to the facilitators by Sister Namibia, and were conducted as focus group discussions in three language groups. The participants thus had the opportunity to monitor and evaluate their own actions, advise and learn from each other in order to perform better in the activities planned for the next part of the Campaign. The evaluation sessions gave the responsibility to the participants to establish criteria for the outcomes and impact of the Campaign, as well as to evaluate what worked and why in the diverse contexts.

The Campaign as a model of democratic practice

The whole campaign can be considered as a model of democratic practice since the various strategies and activities of the Campaign strengthened democratic working relations between the different stakeholders. The broad consultation and active participation by so many diverse women encouraged open discussion of issues and the search for different solutions for different contexts while embarking on a common cause.

Notes

1 See 'Women in politics in Namibia: a situational analysis'. In Women in politics in Southern Africa. WiLDAF, 2000.

2 Hubbard, Dianne, '50/50 Options for Namibia'. Windhoek, 2001. Unpublished paper.

3 DTA and CoD are opposition parties in Namibia.

4 The Namibian, 11 March 2002.

5 Minutes of the Strategic planning workshop for elected women, held 4-5 July 2002, p 16.

Annotated bibliography and web resources

A guide to the bibliography: explanation of the records in the bibliography

The records in the annotated bibliography are listed alphabetically by author with an author and a geographical index, which give the record number within the bibliography. Each record is complemented by an abstract.

Photocopying services: Libraries, organizations as well as individual users from any country in the world may request photocopies of articles and small books (up to 100 pages) included in the bibliography.
Photocopying services for users in developing countries are free-of-charge. Information about charges and library services can be requested at the KIT Information and Library Services (ILS).
Please state the KIT Library code of the book(s), chapter(s) or journal article(s) in your request.

KIT Library and Information Services
KIT (Royal Tropical Institute)
P.O. Box 95001
1090 HA Amsterdam, The Netherlands
Fax: +31 (0) 20 - 6654423
E-mail: library@kit.nl
URL: http://www.kit.nl/ils/

An example of a typical record is shown below:

[1] **004**   [2] **Breaking the shackles: political participation of Hazara women in Afghanistan** [3] EMADI, HAFIZULLAH. [4]*Asian Journal of Women's Studies* 6(2001)10, p. 143-161 [5] ref. [6] ISSN 1225-9276
Afghanistan is a mosaic of various ethno-linguistic communities, each with its unique culture and tradition. Economy, culture, tradition, politics and religious precepts determine the status and role of Women in the public arena, but vary from one ethnic community to the other. This article studies the status and role of women in Afghanistan with regard to their participation in the public arena. It attempts to explain mechanisms of power in Hazaristan and shows that despite an oppressive environment a number of women have successfully gained a prominent status in their respective communities.
KIT Library code [7] 1271-29(2001)10

1) Record number.

2) Original title.

3) All authors are listed and entered in the Author Index.

4) The reference includes the journal title in full (in italics), the volume number, year of publication (in brackets), issue number, inclusive page numbers as stated in the original document. For monographs, the publisher, place, number of pages and year of publication are given.

5) Summaries, glossaries, indexes, illustrations and literature references are also noted.

6) The bibliographic data conclude with the ISSN or ISBN (if available) of the original document.

7) A unique library code, of the book, chapters or journal articles, available in KIT Library, is given at the end of each record. Please state this number in your photocopy request. When it concerns an electronic document, the URL is provided, however, photocopies of these documents are also available at KIT Library.

Annotated bibliography

001 From palm tree to parliament: training women for political leadership and public life
ABDELA, LESLEY. *Gender and Development* 8(2000)3, p. 16-23, 2 lit.refs ISSN 1355-2074
Data compiled by the Inter-Parliamentary Union on the current proportion of women in parliaments around the world revealed that out of a total of 40,052 MPs worldwide, 31,505 were men and 5052 were women. The percentage of women is therefore 13.8%. This absence of women from the political decision making process produces governments that ignore, or even disdain, what women want and need. Until women achieve numbers in legislatures far nearer parity, all advances in equality between women and men must therefore be viewed as extremely fragile. Against this background, the following issues were discussed: (1) barriers to women's leadership: men's and women's views; (2) a holistic response to the problem; (3) the 300-group, an NGO which aims to increase the number of women elected to local councils and parliament in the UK; and (4) lessons learned. It was concluded that the negative attitudes of political parties, governments, the media and the public towards women leaders must change if progress is to be made.
KIT Library code D 3030-8(2000)3

002 Women in conflict, post-conflict, and reconstruction
AFSHAR, HALEH. *Development in Practice* 2/3. Carfax, Basingstoke 156 p. 2003. lit.refs ISSN 0961-4524
Many of the papers published in this special issue were presented at two meetings held at the University of York in 2001 and 2002. The focus is on what happens to women during wars and what their demands are in the subsequent periods of peace and reconstruction Theoretical and practical knowledge is combined to forge more effective measures and suggest changes that could lead to the inclusion of women at all stages of post-war and reconstruction processes. An overview of the situation of women at times of war and peace explores some prevalent myths, including the assumption that there is a war front that is separate from the home front and that women are always victims in times of conflict. Country studies from Kosova, Palestine and Afghanistan are included. It is demonstrated that conflicts can both empower and disempower women, since women can at the same time be included in practice and yet excluded ideologically, or they may be both victims and agents of change, though they often have no effective choice in these matters. Finally, it is shown that peace processes, whether at the local, national or the international level, seldom include the perspectives that emerge from women's shared suffering.
KIT Library code D 2672-13(2003)2/3

003 Promoting gender equity in the democratic process: women's paths to political participation and decision making
AHERN, PATRICIA; NUTI, PAUL; MASTERSON, JULIA M. *Synthesis Paper*. International Center for Research on Women (ICRW), Washington, DC, 2000, 40 p. ill. lit.refs
This synthesis paper established a framework for examining the relationship between good governance and women's empowerment, and reports on the ways that a sample of 14 PROWID ('Promoting Women in Development' grants programme) projects has influenced this connection in specific countries and contexts. All the projects described can be viewed against the backdrop of three core elements, which provide reference points for understanding what happened in the field. These are defined as: political culture, civil society, and government institutions. This paper seeks to reconcile an understanding of key aspects of governance with the widely varied experiences and activities of the women, civil society organizations, and institutions involved in PROWID. Recommendations are presented for practitioners, communities and policymakers regarding how they can better create the

annotated bibliography

conditions necessary for women everywhere to secure equality, fundamental freedoms, and human rights. Lessons learned from PROWID work in the area of democracy and governance are also identified and discussed.

004   Achievements and challenges of women in local governments. Paper presented at the World's Women Congress 2002 organized by the Department of Gender Studies and Development, Makerere University, 21-26 July, 2002
AKIIKI, KURUHIIRA G.M.A. Makerere University, Kampala, 2002
The achievements and challenges of women in leadership in local government in Uganda were examined, drawing on interviews with women councillors from a variety of social, cultural and political backgrounds. The impact of the statutory environment towards women's participation and recognition in the leadership of local governments was also explored. The focus was on the practical level of implementation and the challenges and fears faced by women in local councils when trying to meet the expectations of the electorate. It was concluded that while the current institutional and legal framework has undoubtedly enhanced women's participation in local government, most women at grass-roots level still lack the opportunity to use these provisions due to poverty, ignorance or subordination. Legislation and a supportive environment are therefore not enough: women should be given the ability not just to appreciate the opportunities to take part in leadership but to utilize them and demand more to achieve equality. Women leaders, civil society and the government should also actively promote public awareness, especially among women, of the need to have women in positions of leadership.
URL: http://www.makerere.ac.ug/womenstudies/full%20papers/akiiki.htm

005   Women's organizations in the Arab world
AL-HAMAD, LAILA. *Al-Raida* (2002)97/98, p. 22-27, lit.refs in notes ISSN 0259-9953
Thousands of Egyptian women have neither a birth certificate (BC) nor an identity card (ID). Not being officially registered means that they cannot access basic services such as schooling, credit, the right to vote, and the ability to claim a pension or rights of inheritance when their spouse dies. In 1996, a campaign was launched by a civil society women's organization that redressed this situation. To date approximately 55,000 Egyptian women have obtained IDs and BCs, with roughly 300,000 still in line. Parliament did nothing, illustrating that it is often civil society organizations, not parliament, that lobby for citizen's rights. Arab parliaments are generally perceived as weak, unresponsive institutions resistant to change. They have the lowest levels of female participation in the world 4.6% compared to 12.7% in sub-Saharan Africa. Not surprisingly, women's interests are poorly represented. Against this background, women's day-to-day existence in the Arab world was described, including the challenges and constraints they face. The emergence of women' organizations was examined and their impact on women outlined. It was concluded that while women's organizations are helping to compensat for women's absence from the political sphere and are influencing the status quo, they cannot b expected to be the panacea for resolving women issues in the Arab world.

006   Daughters of the goddess, daughters o imperialism: African women struggle for cultur power and democracy
AMADIUME, IFI. Zed, London, 2000, 300 p. lit.refs ISBN 1-85649-806-9
Transformations in women's organizations are examined through a comparative study of the different contexts in which gender, class and race are dynamic factors. Contradictions in rhetoric and practice as these factors shape women's issues and gender equality work in loca and global contexts in Nigeria, Africa and Britai are analyzed. The focus is on various women's groups and organizations, and the differences in their articulation of women's needs and rights; the formalized nature of the internationally informed language of rights; the 'laundry-list' approach to women's issues in the women and development rhetoric; and the more volatile, combative and subversive language of civil discourse on social justice at the local level. The study then shifts to a structural and institutional perspective that moves beyond formalized rhetoric to contextual contestations of right, thu focusing on concrete situations of women's daily lives and struggle for social justice and the internal fractures and contradictions in the context of western cultural and economic imperialism. The book is therefore about gender class and race relations under the present state system and the contemporary nature of power between different classes of women locally, nationally and globally.

007   Crossing the lines: women's organizations in conflict resolutions
ANDERSON, SHELLEY. *Development* 43(2000)3, p. 34-39, 9 lit.refs ISSN 1011-6370
Women's organizations are playing an increasingly important role in non-violent conflict resolution. They are frequently the first to take the risks necessary to promote dialogue across divided communities and move towards reconciliation. Lack of resources, particularly financial resources, and lack of decision making political power are major obstacles. While women's peace activism challenges many gender stereotypes, there is a danger that women's role in peace-building may also perpetuate such stereotypes.
KIT Library code H 1000-43(2000)3

008   Women, bureaucracy and the governance of poverty in Southeast Asia: integrating gender and participatory governance in poverty reduction programs in the Philippines and Vietnam. Paper presented at the DEVNET international conference on 'Poverty, prosperity, progress', University of Victoria, Wellington, New Zealand, 17-19 November 2000 [Draft]
ANGELES, LEONORA C.
Case studies in 3 villages in the Philippines and Vietnam from 1986 to 1998 explored the relationship between gender planning, good governance and poverty reduction effort. Both have differing policy contexts, political ideological environments, bureaucratic cultures, levels of economic growth and industrialization, women's organizations, and NGOs. The study produced contrasting insights on the integration of gender in state bureaucratic politics in the framing of poverty alleviation plans. Four general conclusions were reached: (1) the implementation of gender-aware programmes is scattered and sporadic; (2) government front line agencies still approach women and gender concerns in a compartmentalized and fragmented manner; (3) confusion exists about women and gender, and the women and development (WID) framework and the gender and development (GAD) framework; and (4) a female presence in state agencies is not synonymous with feminist goals being achieved or gender issues being handled effectively. It was argued that male and female civil servants at all levels need to understand more clearly feminist values and principles of gender equity and empowerment, and how they can effectively bring these into their service work, advocacy roles and work environment. The communities they serve should also understand these values and principles.
URL: http://www.devnet.org.nz/conf/papers/angeles.pdf

009   Asia-Pacific Women Parliamentarians' Conference on Transformative Leadership for Good Governance in the 21st Century, 24-25 March 2000, Bangkok
Center for Asia Pacific Women in Politics (CAPWIP), Paranaque City, 2000
The Asia-Pacific Women Parliamentarians' Conference on Transformative Leadership for Good Governance in the 21st Century' was held in Bangkok, from 24-25 March 2000. The conference was an opportunity for women parliamentarians from the Asia and Pacific region to come together in a forum designed exclusively for them and share their experiences as women who have gained access to positions of decision making and power. The conference is reported in terms of highlights of the 3 plenary sessions, selected papers, common critical points for action drawn from the workshop outputs, and future actions.
URL: http://www.capwip.org/resources/womparlconf2000/toc.htm

010   Gender and local governance in the Philippines
ATIENZA, MARIA ELA L. In: Democracy and the status of women in East Asia ed. by Rose J. Lee, Cal Clark. Rienner, Boulder, CO, 2000, p. 77-90, bibliogr. p. 193-206
Using Sara Longwe's framework for analyzing women's empowerment (UNICEF, 1993), the extent to which women's empowerment has been achieved in the Philippines was assessed in the context of one major aspect of the country's democratization process: the devolution of powers to local governments. The impact of the 1991 Local Government Code was analyzed. However, the primary focus was on some of the initiatives taken by women's organizations, such as the Lipa City Women's Council (LCWC), the Bukidnon Women's Organization, Inc (BWOI), the Democratic Socialist Women of the Philippines (DSWP), the Pan-Cordillera Women's Network for Peace and Development (PAN-CORDI), and the PILIPINA (Movement of Filipino Women) to achieve substantial participation in local governance and affairs. Although some inroads have been made with regard to securing welfare and some levels of empowerment for women, five key problem areas were identified. It was concluded that empowerment should not be confused with the number of women in key positions, but viewed in the context of the collective power of women to contribute effectively to the decision making process. Also, women's groups should look for more sustainable sources of funding and not be co-terminous with any politician's or administration's term of office.
KIT Library code N 00-730

011 Gender, development and democratization in Africa

AUBREY, LISA. In: A decade of democracy in Africa ed. by Stephen N. Ndegwa. International Studies in Sociology and Social *Anthropology* 81. Brill, Leiden, 2001, p. 87-111, 75 lit.refs ISSN 0074-8684

The link between gender, development and democratization in Africa is examined, focusing on ongoing political transitions in Kenya and Ghana. Attention is given to the marginalization of women in the public life of politics, while men continue to both control state structures and determine the neophytes in the public domain. Specific leading women's NGOs in Kenya and Ghana who traverse the public and private domains are looked at, pointing to the artificiality of that dichotomy. It is questioned whether or not this dawn of political change can bring democracy back without women having the same citizenship rights as men. It is demonstrated how this query is relevant in evolving democracies as well as in sustained democracies. The Ghanese and Kenyan cases of women's organizations do not bode well for the making of democratizing women's movements, much less democratizing feminist movements. Instead, they are examples of systems maintaining 'state feminism', defined as 'state-controlled women's organizations and institutions, which address women's issues in a non-threatening way and often against the interests of women'.

012 Women and men in partnership for post-conflict reconstruction: report of the Sierra Leone National Consultation, Free Town, Sierra Leone, May 2001

BAKSH-SOODEEN, RAWWIDA; ETCHART, LINDA. Commonwealth Secretariat, London, 2002, 202 p. ISBN 0-85092-774-7

Following a decade of armed conflict that led to the virtual collapse of the country's social, economic, legal and political fabric, the Sierra Leone national consultation on women and men in partnership for post-conflict reconstruction, held in Freetown in May 2001, brought together 250 people from governmental and non-governmental organizations to discuss ways in which the war has impacted differently on women, children and men, and how to ensure gender equality in all reconstruction efforts. The papers in this report examine the following issues from a gender perspective: political and public decision making; security and peace building; legal reform; violence and other crimes against women and children; poverty, economic recovery and empowerment; health, HIV/AIDS and STIs; resettlement of displaced persons and rehabilitation of ex-combatants; and the role of young people in post-conflict reconstruction.

013 Why women protest: women's movements in Chile

BALDEZ, LISA. *Cambridge Studies in Comparative Politics*. Cambridge University Press, Cambridge, 2002, xvii, 234 p. ill. bibliogr. p 209-225 ISBN 0-521-01006-3

A general framework is used to explain the emergence and evolution of women's protest movements in Chile. The main object of study is the point at which diverse organizations converge to form a women's movement. It is argued that there are two conditions that trigger mobilization among women: partisan realignment, understood as the emergence of a new set of issues around which political elites define themselves, and women's decision to frame realignment in terms of widely held norm about gender difference. These claims are illustrated by two very different women's movements in Chile: the mobilization of women against president Salvador Allende (1970-1973) and the women's movement against General Augusto Pinochet (1973-1990). Despite important differences between these two movements, both emerged amidst a context of partisan realignment and framed their concerns in terms of women's exclusion from the political arena.

014 Gender and nationalism: the masculinization of Hinduism and female politica participation in India

BANERJEE, SIKATA. *Women's Studies International Forum* 26(2003)2, p. 167-179, 48 lit.refs ISSN 0277-5395

Feminist analysis has revealed the gendered nature of nations and nationalism. Adopting such a perspective, the relationship between the masculinization of Hindu nationalism and female political participation was analyzed. The image of an aggressive male warrior is central to certain versions of Hindu nationalism or Hindutva in contemporary India, and is embedded within a political narrative which declares its affinity for ideas of resolute masculinity through an array o symbols, historic icons, and myths. Given that Indian women are very visible in the politics of Hindutva, the way in which women have created a political space for themselves in a very masculine narrative was explored, focusing on the historical and cultural processes that enable this masculinization, certain ideals of femininity implicit within this narrative which opened the door for female participation, and women's use images and icons drawn from a common cultural milieu to enter the political landscape of Hindutva. It was concluded that Indian women have created a space for themselves by casting themselves as warriors, utilizing ideals of nation as woman, and focusing on women's role as mother as well as culturally endorsed ideals of motherhood. They have had to negotiate a delicate balance between seizing a space for themselves and reassuring the male elite that activities playing out in this area will not radically retool culturally dominant ideas of masculinity and femininity in Indian society.

KIT Library code H 2452-26(2003)2

015   Gender and governance: a bibliography
BELL, EMMA. *BRIDGE Bibliography 11*. Institute of Development Studies (IDS), Brighton, 2001
Recent (1995-2001) key materials on a broad range of issues relating to gender and governance are included in this bibliography and presented in 5 sections: (1) general texts on the state and good governance; (2) donor policy documents; (3) effective public management (political regimes, institutionalizing gender, public and financial sector reform, and gender budgets); (4) government accountability (democratization, political representation, electoral systems, decentralization and civil society); and (5) rights policy and the rule of law (international and regional human rights, state policy and the law, and customary law).

URL: http://www.ids.ac.uk/bridge/reports/bb11.pdf

016   National machineries for women in development: experiences, lessons and strategies
BELL, EMMA, et al. *BRIDGE Report 66*. Institute of Development Studies (IDS), Brighton, 2002
This report includes salient points and recommendations from the BRIDGE 1996 report on National Machineries for Women (NWMs, or National Women's Machineries), up-dated with more recent thinking, policy and practice. Also included are summaries of some best practice examples. The original report reviews the experience of national machineries for women in developing countries, drawing on case study material from African, Caribbean and Pacific countries (including Belize, Cameroon, Ethiopia, Jamaica, Namibia, Papua New Guinea, Tonga, Uganda and Zambia) and comparative material from Chile and the Philippines where national machineries are well-established. Background information on NWMs and an overview of constraints to their effectiveness is given. The implications for NWMs of the changing macro-political and institutional environment are explored, emphasizing the current interest in

'good government', in particular programmes of decentralization and civil service reform but also broader issues of participation and democratization. Strategies adopted to further the implementation of gender-aware policy, and case studies are presented.

URL: http://www.ids.ac.uk/bridge/reports/re66.pdf

017   Social cohesion and conflict management: rethinking the issues using a gender-sensitive lens
BESSELL, SHARON. In: Social cohesion and conflict prevention in Asia: managing diversity through development ed. by Nat J. Colletta, Teck Ghee Lim, Anita Kelles-Viitanen. World Bank, Washington, DC, 2001, p. 183-218, lit.refs
Analyses of social cohesion and conflict regularly explore various rifts within society, ethnic-religious, economic, caste-based, and so on, but little attention has been paid to the gender dimensions of these issues. This gap exists despite the greater understanding and the greater capacity to identify not only problems but also solutions that can be gained from a gendered analysis. In an attempt to fill this gap and advance the much-needed debate on this subject, the following questions were asked: why include women; what can women bring; and how do women experience conflict and the aftermath of conflict. It was shown how women's rights are often ignored in times of war and how their contribution to the peace process is also frequently dismissed, as demonstrated during the decade long Bougainvillea conflict in Papua New Guinea and the Blue Ribbon Campaign in Fiji. It was concluded that in order to foster social cohesion, detailed attention to the development of inclusive social policies is necessary. Educational policies too were considered to be vital and should include children from marginalized groups, be sensitive to (minority) languages, and be aware of the important role that teaching history, particularly recent history, can play in promoting tolerance and understanding.

KIT Library code U 01-140

018   Women's roles in conflict prevention, conflict resolution and post-conflict reconstruction: literature review and institutional analysis
BOUTA, T.; FRERKS, G. Netherlands Institute of International Relations 'Clingendael', The Hague, 2003
Women's role in conflict prevention, conflict resolution and post-conflict reconstruction is the focus of this report. It comprises a review of selected literature and an institutional analysis of

16 national and international organizations that aim to improve the position of women in armed conflicts through peace-keeping missions, peace negotiation, peace-building, humanitarian aid, development assistance, and international tribunals and courts. Seven main roles of women before, during and after armed conflict are identified, including women as victims, combatants, peace activists and women in formal peace politics. In practice these roles overlap or coincide, and differ in time and place. Each has challenges and implications for policymakers. The 16 institutions analyzed varied in their mandates, structures, policies, operational procedures and policy implementation, and availability of gender expertise. The International Committee of the Red Cross (ICRC) had significantly mainstreamed gender into its structure by making all employees responsible for taking up gender in their activities. However, they focused mainly on women as victims of conflict and on meeting their practical needs rather than on changes in unequal social relations. Recommendations for the Dutch government included monitoring strategies to see whether women's roles have been strengthened.

URL: http://www.siyanda.org/static/bouta_conflict.htm

019   Women's organizations working for peace and reconciliation in the Great Lakes region of Africa
BOYD, ROSALIND. *Discussion Paper* 90. Centre for Developing-Area Studies, McGill University, Montreal, 2001, 22 p. lit.refs
Women, men and children in war-torn areas are developing various forms of organized resistance to conflict and steps to affirm the possibilities for new lives embedded in a culture of peace. Based on research in the African region and most recently in Rwanda and Uganda in 2000, this document describes some of those initiatives, particularly by women in the Great Lakes region of Africa. It is intended as a resource for those working in the areas of trauma and reconciliation, women and peace-building, and with women's organizations in the Great Lakes region. A brief overview is provided of some key issues related to women and war, and why they must be included in the peace process. Women's experience of conflict is different from that of men, and their needs and benefits from the peace process are also different. It is essential that women are included in and profit from the transition to peace in their community, nation and region. The work of several regional and national organizations is also described. The regional initiatives in Burundi, the Democratic Republic of Congo, Rwanda and Uganda that women have

taken over the decade reflect the importance of transboundary solidarity activities. Women in war-torn countries are forging new alliances to assert their right to be included in the peace-building and development process. The potential contribution of women to political life has yet to be fully realized.

KIT Library code H 1930-(2001)90

020   Reconstructing roles and relations: women's participation in reconstruction in post-Mitch Nicaragua
BRADSHAW, SARAH. *Gender and Development* 9(2001)3, p. 79-87 ISSN 1355-2074
In October 1998, Hurricane Mitch affected 3.5 million people in Central America and left 18,000 dead or missing, the majority in Honduras and Nicaragua. Following the hurricane, many Nicaraguan civil society organizations mobilized themselves to take part in reconstructing the country and to present alternatives to the government's reconstruction plans. The government contributed little to the reconstruction process. The newly-formed Civil Co-ordinator for Emergency and Reconstruction (CCER), a coalition of 350 national NGOs, undertook a large-scale social audit of the reconstruction process. The results of the audit are presented here, together with more in-depth research to provide a gendered analysis of the reconstruction. It focuses on the roles of women in reconstruction, their participation and leadership in reconstruction projects, and individual household responses. It also questions whether reconstruction projects have had any impact on transforming gender relations in post-hurricane communities and points out the need to pay attention to the possible negative indirect impacts of projects designed to 'empower' women.

KIT Library code D 3030-9(2001)3

021   A collection of cases
BROOKFIELD, CHRISTINE. International Union of Local Authorities (IULA), The Hague, 2001
Equality for women is not only a human right, it is essential to good governance and sustainable human settlements. Drawing on case studies from Australia, Canada, Ecuador, Ghana, Guatemala, the Philippines, South Africa, South Korea, Sweden and Turkey, this book reflects the diversity of local actions for gender equality and highlight the various means of promoting it. The case studies do not provide fixed guidelines for local government associations but give different insights into the work of local government associations and examples of innovative practice. Some cases look at national or sub-national

mechanisms, including representation, gender mainstreaming, and gender budgeting. Others address action at the grass-roots level, through cooperation with local groups. Together the cases illustrate the importance of equal representation of and by women in local government.

URL: http://www.iula-int.org/iula/upload/template/templatedocs/womenbrochureiula.pdf

022   Democratization and the Tanzanian state: emerging opportunities for achieving women's empowerment

BROWN, ANDREA M. *Canadian Journal of African Studies* 35(2001)1, p. 67-98, 24 lit.refs ISSN 0008-3968

Tanzania's steps towards political and economic liberalization began in the mid-1980s with structural adjustment, new political openings and the resignation of President Nyerere. Subsequent reforms dramatically affected the country's politics, its economy and its social and cultural fabric. The massive increase in the number of opportunities opening up for urban women to take on new economic and associational roles was examined, drawing on the results of fieldwork in Dar es Salaam in 1996, during which a total of 177 interviews were conducted with women from professional associations, the informal sector, and the political arena. The relatively higher representation of women in Tanzanian politics was attributed to the presence of the government's affirmative action programme. However, once in power, how far will these women push for women's issues at the risk of jeopardizing their own job security? These and other issues were explored, particularly the activities and achievements of different women's groups in Tanzania. It was concluded that the strong civil society now present in Tanzania is largely due to the efforts of women's groups and that while the reform process may have halted, it will have difficulty going in reverse.

KIT Library code A 2201-35(2001)1

023   Gender budgets: what's in it for NGOs?

BUDLENDER, DEBBIE. *Gender and Development* 10(2002)3, p. 82-87, 4 lit.refs ISSN 1355-2074

Gender budget work focuses on the impact of government budgets on women and men, boys and girls, and different sub-groups of the above such as rich and poor, black and white, rural and urban, and young and old. Interest in gender budget work has increased worldwide in the last seven years. Today, over 50 countries have had gender budget initiatives of one kind or another. However, large differences exist between countries: sometimes the initiatives have been located inside government, and sometimes in parliament or even civil society. Just what do gender budgets entail and why would NGOs be interested in engaging in them? These questions were explored in detail and issues such as what gender budget work is (and what it is not), where to start, who does the work, how to be taken seriously and the common dangers, examined. It was concluded that the true value of gender budget projects will only be felt when they manage to convince the sceptics, and this can only be achieved through hard work based on sound facts and figures.

KIT Library code D 3030-10(2002)3

024   Gender budgets make cents: understanding gender responsive budgets

BUDLENDER, DEBBIE, et al. Commonwealth Secretariat, London, 2002

Gender-responsive budget (GRB) initiatives are intended to afford a mechanism by which governments, in collaboration with lawmakers, civil society groups, donor and other development agencies, can integrate a gender analysis into fiscal policies and budgets. A gender-responsive budget is not a separate budget for women but an attempt to disaggregate expenditure and revenue according to their different impacts on women and men. This publication presents a comprehensive review of GRB initiatives. Divided into four sections, it provides a conceptual and theoretical framework, traces the evolution of work in this area, assesses the role of different stakeholders, and highlights lessons learned to date. A profile of known activities at the country level shows how gender-responsive budgets are being used as a pivotal tool with which to assess budgetary performance and impact. The positive benefits that have emerged include an enhanced ability to determine the real value of resources targeted towards gender-specific groups; the challenges to notions of 'gender-neutrality' of many policies and programmes; and strengthening of the collection and analysis of gender-disaggregated data. Suggestions are given for strengthening GRB initiatives for implementation on a wider scale.

URL: http://www.thecommonwealth.org/gender/htm/publications/gms_pdf/GBMC%201%20Understanding%20GB.pdf

025   Gender budgets make more cents: country studies and good practice

BUDLENDEER, DEBBIE; HEWITT, GUY. Commonwealth Secretariat, London, 2002, 194 p. ISBN 0-85092-734-X

This report documents good practice in gender budget work from across the globe. Practitioners share their first-hand experiences and in-depth knowledge of the why, where and how of gender-responsive budget (GRB) initiatives. They reflect on both the challenges, successes and initiatives in the Andean region, Australia, Korea, Mexico, the Philippines, Rwanda, Scotland, South Africa and the UK. A chapter on the Commonwealth Secretariat's involvement in developing and implementing GRB initiatives is also included to suggest the role that can be played by external agencies at the national, regional and international level.

URL: http://www.thecommonwealth.org/pdf/gender/ GBMC%202%20Country%20studies.pdf

KIT Library N 03-1010

026   Building women's capacity to participate in governance. Paper presented for the conference on capacity building North and South links and lessons, 1-3 July, 1999
BUTEGWA, FLORENCE. Associates for Change, Kampala
Following an analysis of what the terms governance and development really mean to developing countries, the case was presented in support of enhancing women's participation in governance. It was argued that women's participation in decision making at the different levels of governance is a development imperative as women represent over half the population and have real expertise and perspectives that would enrich policy formulation and implementation. However, existing social, political and economic situations hold them back. In African countries, this situation is further exacerbated by the legal system and decision making structures. Reform is therefore vital if women are to be included. Uganda was held up as a positive role model in this regard. Finally, appropriate programmes to sensitize the public and increase their legal literacy, coupled with programmes to enhance women's own preparedness and skills in mobilization and alliance building, were also deemed necessary. Women in Africa are capable but individually they cannot move the entrenched systems that work against them.

URL: http://www.associatesforchange.com/ alternative.pdf

027   Democratization and women's grassroots movements
BYSTYDZIENSKI, JILL M.; SEKHON, JOTI. Kali for Women, New Delhi, 2002, vii, 397 p. lit.refs
ISBN 81-86706-54-2
Attention for democratic movements worldwide has focused on national activities, electoral politics and the expansion of capitalist markets, whereas the connections between women's grass-roots organizations and democratization have been neglected. This book studies the contribution of these movements to the expansion of public and private spaces and democratic processes. The 16 case studies of women's grass-roots movements in India, Hong Kong, Singapore, Eritrea, South Africa, Syria, Egypt, El Salvador, Honduras, Poland, Russia, Belgium, Ireland, Canada, the USA (Appalachia) and Australia reveal the connections between local political and social action, and the growth of democratic processes at state, regional and global levels. They illustrate how community-based actions, programmes and organizations that empower women contribute to the creation of a civil society and thus enhance democracy. Theoretical and practical implications for democratization of the most salient issues raised by the case studies are discussed, including the expansion of spaces for participation by women at many levels; the factors that enhance or limit the participatory democratic process, such as the relationship between grass-roots women's groups and the state, the dominant groups and interests within the country, the structure of women's organizations, and the differences and divisions among women; women's varying ideas regarding feminism; and the effects of globalization.

KIT Library code P 02-1860

028   Women and democratization: lessons from Latin America
CAGAN, ELIZABETH. *Advances in Gender Research* (2000)4, p. 91-121, bibliogr. p. 116-121
By 1995, more than a dozen dictatorships in Latin America were replaced by elected governments. For the first time in history, civilian rule and constitutional government was the norm. Yet these developments were surprising since they occurred in both the poorest and richest nations of the region, and during a period of economic instability, not the best time for democratic reform. It was against this background that the following question was explored: has the advancement of democracy in Latin America, which helps emancipate citizens in general, also furthered the emancipation of women in particular. Issues explored in pursuit of an answer to this question included: the contribution of international development programmes to women's empowerment; neoliberalism and women in Latin America; women in Latin American social movements; maintaining war-time gains for women; a case study of women's empowerment in El Salvador; women and democracy; and the decline of the welfare state. It was concluded that democracy has opened up a space for women and other disenfranchised

groups in the region to play a more formal role in the political affairs of their nations, but this opening has been weakened by the declining potency of conventional politics.

029   Gender budgets and beyond: feminist fiscal policy in the context of globalisation
ÇAGATAY, NILÜFER. In: Women reinventing globalisation ed. by Joanna Kerr and Caroline Sweetman. *Gender and Development* 11(2003)1, p. 15-24, 24 lit.refs ISSN 1355-2074
Macro-economic theories and macro-economic policies in general, and fiscal policies in particular, are rarely gender-neutral. Since the mid-1980s, gender budget analysis, which has been undertaken in many countries, has been a key strategy to challenge macro-economic theorising and policymaking. Such initiatives, along with a variety of pro-poor budget initiatives, constitute the major challenge to the prevailing fiscal policy stance in many countries. The changes in the fiscal policy stance in the context of liberalization and globalization were discussed here in order to draw out their implications for social inequality, especially gender inequality. Many liberalization policy programmes have led to a fiscal squeeze by putting pressure on public budgets. In addition, market liberalization has eroded public revenues, and economic insecurity and vulnerability are on the increase. Issues such as the implications of fiscal retrenchment for growth, development and equality; the gender implications of liberalization; the gender bias in economic crises and its impact on women; and democratizing fiscal policy and increasing accountability to women were analyzed. A variety of policy advocacy positions open to feminist activists were presented, through which they could build on the work of gender budget initiatives.

030   Militarism, warfare and the search for peace in Angola: the contribution of Angolan women
CAMPBELL, HORACE. *Occasional Paper* 63. Africa Institute of South Africa, Pretoria, 2001, 43 p. ill. lit.refs ISBN 0-7983-0144-9
This analysis of warfare and militarism in Angola seeks to deconstruct the ethnic narrative that has been pronounced. It starts from the perspective that if all of the peace accords have failed, there needs to be more critical attention paid to the intellectual and social basis for warfare. Not only the physical violence that is visited on this society is explored, but also the social and structural violence. An effort is made to penetrate militarism so that the alternatives of demilitarization and peace can be grasped beyond conciliating military forces. The conclusion seeks to centralize the place of Angolan men and women in the search for peace. In an attempt to rise above the androcentricism of traditional political science, the paper focuses on the central role of women in the search for peace.

031   Self-governance, political participation and the feminist movement in South Korea
CHIN, MIKYUNG. In: Democracy and the status of women in East Asia ed. by Rose J. Lee, Cal Clark. Rienner, Boulder, CO, 2000, p. 91-104, ill. bibliogr. p.193-206
The expansion of women's rights and the exponential growth of the women's movement in South Korea is remarkable considering the long history of well-defined unequal gender roles in traditional Korean society. Yet, despite this progress, the status of women is far from satisfactory when set against the ideal of perfect equality with men, especially in the political arena. Rising divorce rates and juvenile delinquency have also encouraged an anti-feminist backlash urging women's return to the family. In an effort to understand the pitfalls that accompanied the feminist movement following democratization, issues such as the historical context of patriarchal Confucianism; the history of the women's movement in South Korea; and local self-governance and women's political representation were analyzed. New directions for Korean feminism were also examined. It was concluded that the feminist movement in South Korea must rid itself of its 'anti-family' image and devise more subtle strategies to gain men's support rather than alienating them.

032   Women and democracy: a Bangladesh perspective
CHOUDHURY, DILARA. *Round Table* (2000)357, p. 563-576, lit.refs in notes ISSN 0035-8533
Since the re-establishment of liberal democracy in Bangladesh in 1991, the country has been struggling hard for the consolidation of its tenuous existence. It has been an uphill task in the face of seemingly insurmountable obstacles. In the meantime, the impact of globalization and internal social forces have brought other democratic concerns to the fore. Various strategies such as the feminist movement, both liberal as well as socialist, the roles of the NGOs and the state are analyzed. In conclusion, attempts are made to evaluate those factors

which have given more prominence to the women's agenda. It is argued that women's demands in Bangladesh, under the rubric of a more participatory democracy, are still far from reality. A lot needs to be done to make feminist voices heard so that the democratic base of the country can be broadened.

033   A study of the San Salvador municipal gender equity policy
CLULOW, MICHAEL. *Gender Equity and Local Governance, Building Women's Citizenship and Governance, Central America*. One World Action, London, 2003
In 1999 the San Salvador Municipal Council approved the Municipal Gender Equity Policy and thereby became the first municipality in El Salvador to formalize and institutionalize its commitment to gender equity in an integrated way. This paper reports on the process of developing and implementing the policy which provides valuable lessons for the promotion of women's rights and their participation as citizens, not only through local government but at all levels. One of the factors that has facilitated the approval and implementation of the Municipal Gender Equity Policy has been the determined and persistent action of the women's movement and the commitment of women councillors. In addition, the Council's citizens' participation policy helped to promote dialogue with women while funding from international aid agencies made the implementation of many activities possible. The most important impacts so far within the Council include the legitimization of gender equity as a theme for council action and changes in attitudes.
URL: http://www.oneworldaction.org/download/san_salvador_eng_a4.pdf

034   Making spaces, changing places: situating participation in development
CORNWALL, ANDREA D. *IDS Working Paper* 170. University of Sussex. Institute of Development Studies (IDS), Brighton, 2002, 35 p. lit.refs ISSN 1353-6141 ISBN 1-85864-472-0
There has been a growing interest in ways to enhance public involvement in governance, and with it the quality and legitimacy of democratic decision making. In addition to conventional models of political participation, a new architecture of democratic practice is developing. Whether in budgeting, policy dialogue, project appraisal, monitoring or evaluation, participatory alternatives to expert-driven processes have gained ground. Using the concept of space as a lens through which to view

practices of participation, this paper seeks to explore issues of power and difference in the making and shaping of spaces for participation in development. It examines the emergence of different kinds of spaces for participation in development, highlighting salient tracks and traces in previous times and their imprint on contemporary practice. The dynamics and dimensions of participation in institutionalized and non-institutionalized spaces, both those of invited participation and more organically created spaces, made and shaped by people for themselves are examined. It is concluded that enhancing citizenship participation requires more than inviting or inducing people to participate. Effective participation requires giving people access to information on which to base deliberation or to mobilize to assert their rights and accountability.

035   Preparing the grounds for a new local politics: the case of women in two African municipalities
DAUDA, CAROL L. *Canadian Journal of African Studies* 35(2001)2, p. 246-281, 50 lit.refs ISSN 0008-3968
A comparison was made between the decentralization programmes of Uganda and Zimbabwe during an eight-month study carried out in 1995 as part of a doctoral thesis. It was concluded that women's participation in local politics is an important indicator of the conscious attempt to meet the challenge of overcoming some of the inherited political impediments of the bifurcated state and changing the relations that shape its political power. In Uganda, the changing consciousness with regard to gender relations was accompanied by a consciousness of the need to democratize at the local level in order to produce new political behaviour. This was not the case in Zimbabwe, where women were systematically excluded from politics except in their capacity to support despotic political power. A definitive difference was also found between the one party dominance of ZANU(PF) in Zimbabwe and the no-party thrust of Uganda's movement system. The deep conservatism within ZANU(PF), both in its officials' attitude towards women's participation and in their attempt to shape women's political behaviour revealed how instrumental the party apparatus was in retaining political power through perpetuating despotic power relations locally. Clearly, it is crucial to observe how women participate in local politics in order to better understand how political change is taking place in sub-Saharan Africa.

gender, citizenship and governance

036   Are women really the 'fairer' sex? Corruption and women in government
DOLLAR, DAVID; FISMAN, RAYMOND; GATTI, ROBERTA. *Policy Research Report on Gender and Development Working Paper Series* 4. World Bank, Washington, DC, 1999, 15 p. ill. lit.refs
Numerous behavioural studies have found that women are more trust-worthy and public-spirited than men. These findings suggest that increasing the direct participation of women in government could serve to mitigate some of the problems associated with government, including corruption. In this paper an attempt is made to analyze the relation between female participation in government legislatures and the level of perceived corruption in a sample of more than 100 countries. As principal measure of corruption the International Country Risk Guide's corruption index is used. The results suggest that there may be extremely important spin-offs stemming from increasing female representation: if women are less likely then men to behave opportunistically, then bringing more women into government may have significant benefits for society in general.
KIT Library code K 3101-(1999)4

037   Women and governance from the grassroots in Melanesia
DOUGLAS, BRONWEN. *State, Society and Governance in Melanesia: Discussion Paper* 2. Australian National University. Research School of Pacific and Asian Studies, Canberra, 2000, 31 p. ill. lit.refs
The papers in this collection are edited versions of contributions to a State, Society and Governance in Melanesia Project workshop on 'Women, Christians, citizens: being female in Melanesia today,' held at Sorrento, Victoria, in November 1998. They address programmes and strategies to enhance the skills, self-respect and community status and effectiveness of rural women in a Melanesian nation-state. Several papers outline policy implications of the case studies discussed, and all make compelling arguments for the civic, social and moral importance of encouraging and tapping the capacities of village women. Religion appears to be central to Melanesian individual and collective lives, and it is attributed practical efficacy and spiritual significance. All the women's organizations, programmes and strategies discussed have strong church links, either direct or de facto via funding, training and personnel. In Melanesia, church women's wings and village women's groups continue to provide women's main opportunities for training, leadership, solidarity, networking and wider experience

beyond the village and even beyond national borders. Policymakers should take Christianity seriously as a powerful cultural element in Melanesian governance, beyond the institutional frameworks for local administration and aid delivery provided by church organizations, regarded as NGOs.
KIT Library code H 2557-(2000)2

038   Mainstreaming women into NEPAD: invisible progress?
DUPREE, LILA; OGUNSANYA, KEMI. *Peace and Government Programme Briefing Paper* 8, 2003
The New Partnership for African Development (NEPAD) is an African initiative that focuses on increasing private sector funding, appealing to Western standards of good governance. With regards to the needs and interests of women, the G8 African Action Plan states that they will 'support African efforts to achieve equal participation of African women in all aspects of the NEPAD process and in fulfilling the NEPAD objectives with regards to peace and security issues'. This paper addresses concerns about women and NEPAD, and suggests recommendations towards mainstreaming women into the initiative. The role of donor agencies, women's groups, NGOs and international agencies is also looked at.
URL: http://www.ai.org.za/monographs/paper82003.html

039   Breaking the shackles: political participation of Hazara women in Afghanistan
EMADI, HAFIZULLAH. *Asian Journal of Women's Studies* 6(2000)1, p. 143-161, 12 lit.refs
ISSN 1225-9276
Afghanistan is a mosaic of various ethno-linguistic communities, each with its unique culture and tradition. Economy, culture, tradition, politics and religious precepts determine the status and role of women in the public arena, but vary from one ethnic community to the other. This article studies the status and role of women in Afghanistan with regard to their participation in the public arena. It attempts to explain mechanisms of power in Hazaristan and shows that, despite an oppressive environment, a number of women have succeeded in gaining a prominent status in their respective communities.
KIT Library code H 2260-6(2000)1

040   Empowerment and poverty reduction: a sourcebook
Poverty Reduction and Economic Management (PREM), World Bank, 2002 [Draft]
A growing body of evidence is showing the linkages between empowerment and good

governance and growth that is more pro-poor, and improved project performance. However, there remain many questions about what empowerment means, how it applies to the World Bank's work, and what actions should be undertaken to move the empowerment agenda forward. This sourcebook addresses these issues, taking into account the World Bank's mandate and comparative advantage in this field. It focuses on applications in five areas: (1) access by poor people to basic services; (2) improved local governance; (3) improved national governance and economy-wide reform; (4) pro-poor market development; and (5) access by poor people to justice.

URL: http://www.worldbank.org/poverty/empowerment/sourcebook/draftsum.pdf

041   Impact of government budgets on poverty and gender equality. Final draft. Paper prepared for the inter-agency workshop on improving the effectiveness of integrating gender into government budgets, London, 26-27 April 2000
ESIM, SIMEL. International Centre for Research on Women (ICRW), Washington, DC
Three macro-economic policies must be considered when thinking about government budgets: exchange rate policy, monetary policy and fiscal policy. Until recently, most gender-sensitive budget initiatives have focused on the expenditure side of budgets. Yet the assessments of different gender-sensitive budget initiatives suggest a need to gain ground on the revenue side. Against this background, the expenditure and revenue statements of fiscal policy as strategic entry points for engendering macro-economics were examined. This was followed by a discussion of the potential implications of monetary policy and overall fiscal stance on poverty and gender equality. Transfers (pensions, unemployment benefits), subsidies (agricultural products, food, export) and services (public goods and utilities such as law and order, health, education, electricity) were the three categories of public spending discussed as they affect the poor and women. Two research tools were also reviewed, benefit incidence and time use studies, and their applications to gender budget analysis examined. Tax incidence studies, the impact of user fees, the gender implications of tax reform, and the impact of globalization on revenue were all explored with examples from around the world, such as the popular response to debt relief in Bolivia, taxing suitcase traders, and alcohol tax in India.

URL: http://www.siyanda.org/docs/future_direction.doc

042   Guide to launching a national campaign for 50/50 in government
ESPINE-VILLALUZ, SHEILA; REYES, MELANIE M. Center for Legislative Development (CLD), Pasig City, 2001, 41 p. ill. lit.refs
Although women have taken an unprecedented active role in political events around the world in the last decade, the fact remains that women are and continue to be under-represented, if not invisible, in decision making at all levels of governance. To concretely address the issue of women's under-representation in power structures and decision making, WEDO (Women's Environment and Development Organization) launched a global campaign in June 2000 calling for '50-50 by 2005: Women in Government — Get the Balance Right.' The campaign specifically demands that governments work for a 'provisional minimum target of 30% representation of women in cabinet ministries and legislatures as well as local authorities by 2003 and equal representation by 2005.' It emphasizes the importance of setting numerical, time-specific targets to ensure that governments translate their words and commitments in action. Having explained the need for gender balance in government, this guide provides practical steps to launch a national 50-50 campaign.
KIT Library code Br N 02-516

043   The first step: getting in the door. WEDO Primer 50/50 Campaign Women's Environment and Development Organization (WEDO) <www.wedo.org>, New York, NY, 2001
On 8 June 8 2000, WEDO launched a campaign called '50/50 by 2005: get the balance right!' that challenges governments to take action to increase women's political participation. WEDO's 50/50 campaign, endorsed by more than 170 organizations in 52 countries, has been designed to confront the structural and cultural barriers that impede women's access to decision making and leadership positions. It sets targets for governments: 30% representation of women in cabinet ministries, legislatures and local government by 2003, and equal representation by 2005. This document presents a series of edited texts from the June 8 launch. In bringing together the voices of the women present at the event, it reveals the groundwork for improving women's participation in political systems that is being done in Europe, France, Sweden, the Philippines, Japan, South Africa, India, Egypt, Croatia, Uganda, Germany, Australia, Trinidad & Tobago, Namibia, Nigeria, Kenya and Argentina. The goal of political equality for women, half of all seats at all levels, is the same no matter what country or form of government, but that getting

gender, citizenship and governance

there is a process that will filter through different political systems, cultural norms and varying degrees of commitment on the part of governments and societies. The women who spoke reflected the differences, both in their achievements and in their strategies for change.
URL: http://www.iula-int.org/iula/upload/docs/womenandgovernment-50-50campaign (wedoprimer2001).doc

044 **Beyond the barricades: women, civil society, and participation after democratization in Latin America**
FITZSIMMONS, TRACY. *Comparative Studies in Democratization*. Garland, New York, NY, 2000, xvii, 205 p. ill. bibliogr.: p. 189-202
ISBN 0-8153-3736-1
It is examined how the emergence of new democracies affects the organized participation of citizens. Prominent theorists assume that a transition to democracy paradoxically demobilizes civil society, leading to a disbanding of organizations and a decline in participation. This book challenges these assumptions and demonstrates that the story is more complex. First, while political participation is reduced significantly, citizens continue to participate actively in the social, economic and cultural realms following a transition to democracy. At the same time, most political organizations and their membership remain structurally and hierarchically intact, largely inactive except in crisis situations. There is therefore an organizational residue in the political realm. Second, groups with a common goal and a common identity may seem most likely to survive, but instead they may be among the weakest and may conform to the demobilization hypothesis. In the Chilean example, while many women have left the household, women's groups have failed to occupy the public space; feminist organizations may have been successful in getting women to participate, but their participation has been largely outside the traditionally political realm. These findings have implications for the stability, type and quality of democracy. The findings imply that those who study civil society by concentrating on the regime level and on national social movements miss a sizable portion of the action. With decentralization a growing reality, scholars must look to the local level in order to understand participation after democratization.
KIT Library code P 01-124

045 **Fostering women's participation in development through non-governmental efforts in Cameroon**
FONJONG, LOTSMART. *Geographical Journal* 167(2001)3, p. 223-234, ill. 23 lit.refs
ISSN 0016-7398
Women constitute 52% of the population of Cameroon and a play a crucial role in the development of society at all levels. Unfortunately, they function from a subordinate position inherent in both traditional and state institutions. Women's empowerment is currently an issue of national concern and both state and international efforts at mainstreaming women in development have so far produced mixed results. The grass-roots approach of NGOs has been effective in reaching women at all levels. Activities of NGOs have had far reaching but mixed effects in meeting both practical and strategic gender needs. Case studies of NGOs and women's empowerment in Cameroon are examined and their successes, with regard to improved access and welfare, and their limitations, with regard to conscientization, participation and control, are highlighted.
KIT Library code E 1879-167(2001)3

046 **Unfinished transitions: women and the gendered development of democracy in Venezuela, 1936-1996**
FRIEDMAN, ELISABETH J. Pennsylvania State University Press, University Park, PA, 2000, xix, 324 p. ill. bibliogr.: p. 295-315 ISBN 0-271-02024-5
The women's movement during the process of democratization in Venezuela is analyzed with a focus on the interaction between women's organizations and formal political institutions, including the socio-economic and political changes in women's status during the period under study, the general and gender-based political opportunities of the period, the development of women's organizing and interests, and women's principal moments of mobilization. The experiences of women's groups during liberalized authoritarianism (1936-1945) and the first transitions to democracy (1945-1948) reveal how the political parties have institutionalized and legitimized gender bias. Women's participation against dictatorship (1948-1958) led to their increasing mobilization at its fall. The gender-specific impact of party-driven democratization has been an important factor of women's demobilization in the next transition (1958-1974). Women's organizing advanced in the consolidation of democracy (1974-1984) taking advantage of the opportunity offered by the UN Decade for Women (1975-1985). Women's most successful period of mobilization has been 1984-

1990, when they were able to implement the lessons drawn from their long history of organizing. The effects of economic and political crises on women's organizing efforts (1989-1995) are highlighted. The book concludes with a reflection on the potential for women's transformation from anti-authoritarian activists to full-fledged players in the interest-group politics of consolidated democracies.

KIT Library code P 00-1656

047 Gender and armed conflict

BRIDGE Cutting Edge Pack. Institute of Development Studies (IDS), Brighton, 2003
Adverse effects of armed conflict on gender equality and ways in which these inequalities might be overcome are explored in this pack, comprising an overview paper, a collection of resource materials such as key texts, case studies and tools, and a bulletin that includes articles on the issue.

URL: http://www.ids.ac.uk/bridge/
reports_gend_CEP.html

048 Gender and budgets

Gender and Development in Brief 12. Institute of Development Studies (IDS), Brighton, 2003
While government budgets have allocated resources in a way that has perpetuated gender biases, budgets also offer the potential to transform gender inequalities. In recent years, gender budget initiatives (GBIs) have risen to this challenge. Although most GBIs are still primarily focused on analyzing the budget and its impact, the ultimate aim is to mainstream gender into the criteria for its formulation. This issue on 'Gender and Budgets' features an overview of GBIs as a tool to advance towards gender equality. Two case studies are presented; one addressing women's involvement in the formulation of the budget in the municipality of Recife, Brazil; the other drawing on the Tanzania Gender Networking Programme to show that extra political leverage can come from coalitions of civil society organizations.

KIT Library code D 3654-(2003)12
URL: http://www.ids.ac.uk/bridge/dgb12.html

049 Gender, citizenship and governance programme: guide for action research and developing good practice

Royal Tropical Institute (KIT), Amsterdam, 2001, 27 p.
The Gender, Citizenship and Good Governance (GCG) programme initiated by the Royal Tropical Institute (KIT) aims to make gender equity and equality a core concern in the debate on and the practice of good governance globally. It is a framework to facilitate innovative gender and governance initiatives in South Asia and Southern Africa. This guide has been developed for the specific context of the GCG programme and is to be used by the partners in the programme, and the regional and KIT coordinators. It provides direction and facilitation for the action research component of the programme to develop a uniform approach to documenting, monitoring and reporting of the action research projects. Also included is a description of the key theoretical premises, including gender, citizenship and governance, and their operationalization in the context of the CGC programme.

KIT Library code Br G 01-296

050 Gender mainstreaming action plan. Public version

Department for Disarmament Affairs (DDA), United Nations (UN), New York, NY
This document contains excerpts from the internal action plan of the Department for Disarmament Affairs (DDA) to implement a mainstreaming strategy in support of gender equality. The original document was drafted for internal use by DDA. Some chapters, in particular chapter 2 outlining the goals of the action plan, reflect the strategy of DDA. Checklists for organizing a panel, the conduct of fact-finding missions, the preparation of briefing notes and the formulation of project proposals are included. The annexes provide background information and food for thought in the ongoing challenge to identify ways and opportunities to simultaneously work for disarmament and gender equality.

URL: http://disarmament.un.org/gender/gmap.pdf

051 Getting the balance right: strategies for change. WEDO Primer: Women in Government 2

Women's Environment and Development Organization (WEDO), New York, NY, 2001
Women face formidable obstacles to participation in government, many of which stem from deeply rooted patriarchal structures and societal attitudes. They are still often considered unequal to men, in the workplace, at home, in government, and are assigned roles accordingly. The reports presented here reveal the various organizational strategies women are using to overcome the barriers to their political participation. These strategies include gender-sensitive campaign training for women candidates, demanding party quotas to broaden women's electoral participation and providing support services to women legislators at the local and national levels. In Trinidad and Tobago, the

campaign training programme of the Network of Women's NGOs emphasizes the acquisition and development of political skills, as well as gender analysis of budget allocations and local government laws, history and functions. The reports on Sweden and South Africa illustrate the extent to which party quotas and proportional representation contribute to raising the numbers of women in national parliaments. In the Philippines, women activists are helping women legislators develop the technical skills needed to formulate a realistic and prioritized gender-based legislative agenda. The reports show that such alliances enable elected women to navigate the legislative process, participate actively and make meaningful interventions in committee and floor deliberations, while encouraging them to involve their constituents in decision making.

URL: http://www.iula-int.org/iula/upload/docs/womenand government2-50-50campaign(wedoprimer2001).doc

052 Rural women leadership

GHOSH, BHOLA NATH. Mohit, New Delhi, 2002, xiii, 124 p. ill. lit.refs ISBN 81-7445-180-3
Since 1993 women's representation in Gram Panchayats in India has increased due to reservation of seats which was included in the of 73rd Amendment to the Constitution. Based on studies in 2 districts of West Bengal, the role of rural women in Gram Panchayats is assessed. Women's awareness, their participation in the different activities and their ability to take decisions in different public affairs are analyzed. It is shown that the 1993 election in West Bengal was held on the basis that one-third of the total members in each tier of the Panchayats would be reserved for women. This reservation enabled women to participate in the self-government bodies in greater number. Before 1993 women also participated in the elected Panchayats in West Bengal, but then their number was far fewer than the participating men. From 1993, women's participation has become more pronounced (at least 33% due to reservation) in the Panchayats and has been incorporated into active political and social work.
KIT Library code P 03-567

053 Gender-sensitive local auditing: initiatives from India to build accountability to women

GOETZ, ANNE MARIE; JENKINS, ROB. Development Outreach 3(2001)2, p. 18-20, 3 lit.refs ISSN 1020-797X
Financial auditing is usually seen as the preserve of skilled officials so poor people, particularly women, do not normally scrutinize government spending at the local level. However, several state and civil society initiated efforts in India are engaging the poor, especially women, in closer scrutiny of local spending and policy implementation. The aim is to enhance public-sector accountability by exposing incidents of poorly targeted spending and outright corruption. In practice, however, poor people often encounter fierce resistance when they challenge local decision making and spending patterns, especially when the interests of local elites and officials are threatened. Cases from Kerala and Rajasthan were cited where corrupt politicians, officials and shopkeepers used a variety of tactics to sabotage the auditing process, such as intimidation, withholding information, and trickery. It was concluded that legislation alone is not the answer. If citizen-based monitoring and auditing is to work, it needs strong and consistent backing from public sector allies and social movement support.
KIT Library code K 3046-3(2001)2

054 No shortcuts to power: constraints on women's political effectiveness in Uganda

GOETZ, ANNE MARIE. Journal of Modern African Studies 40(2002)4, p. 549-575, 25 lit.refs ISSN 0022-287X
Fixed quotas of seats for women in Uganda's parliament and local government boosted the number of women in public office after the introduction of the National Resistance Movement's (NRM) 'no party system'. By June 2001, 25% of Members of Parliament (MPs) and 30% of local councillors were women. Between 1998 and 2000 in-depth interviews and group discussions were held with MPs, local government councillors, and various activists and academics in order to assess the impact of this affirmative action on women's political effectiveness. The extent to which women MPs have been able to advance gender equity concerns in key new legislation and how far women have benefited (or lost) from the suspension of party competition in Uganda's 'no party' democracy was also analyzed. Fixed quotas were simply 'added on' to the standard number of seats, more as an afterthought, and that the pay-off for the NRM for this affirmative action was an expanded vote bank. This arrangement undermined women's effectiveness once in office because the gate-keepers of access to reserved political space were not the women's movement, or even women voters, but Movement elites. The women's movement in Uganda has become increasingly critical of the deepening authoritarianism of the NRM, pointing out that its failure to follow constitutional commitments to gender equity through to changes in key new

pieces of legislation affecting women's rights is due to its own lack of internal democracy.

KIT Library code A 1995-40(2002)4

055   In and against the party: women's representation and constituency-building in Uganda and South Africa
GOETZ, ANNE MARIE; HASSIM, SHIREEN. In: Gender justice, development, and rights ed. by Maxine Molyneux and Shahra Razavi. Oxford University Press for UNRISD, Oxford, 2002, p. 306-343, 54 lit.refs
Women's relationship to political parties in South Africa and Uganda is explored by looking at the effects of processes and consequences of transitions from authoritarianism on women's political participation in representative institutions. One of the characteristics of transitions from authoritarianism in the two countries has been an increase in the numbers of women in national and local politics. In both countries, the ruling political parties have recognized the importance of women as a political constituency and the importance of women's representation as a key component of citizen participation. However, it is the differences, rather than the similarities, between the two polities that are instructive for an understanding of the institutional forms that could facilitate effective representation of women's political and economic interests, and the political conditions under which representational politics might be used to advance a feminist agenda. The effectiveness of the strategies and discourses used by the women's movements in Uganda and South Africa for inclusion in the dominant parties, and the impact on gender equity in parties and in national policies are assessed. It appears that pluralism in South Africa and a dominant party which is socially inclusive and committed to fighting social inequalities have meant that women can use electoral processes to build leverage behind their political and policy ambitions. The lack of either pluralism or internal party democracy in Uganda has meant that women are dangerously dependent on presidential patronage for access to office and for promoting gender equity policies.

KIT Library code U 03-21

056   No shortcuts to power: African women in politics and policy making
GOETZ, ANNE MARIE; HASSIM, SHIREEN. *Democratic Transition in Conflict-torn Societies* 3. Zed, London, 2003, x, 246 p. ill. lit.refs ISBN 1-84277-147-7
In Uganda and South Africa, women inserted gender equality as a core principle in the new constitution. They have also made their way in unprecedented numbers into the legislature and into local government at all levels. They have done so in different ways. In South Africa a strong women's movement has exploited the competitive dynamic of party politics to assert leverage in electoral struggles, while in Uganda women have benefited from presidential patronage and the creation of new representative offices for women-only competition. This book focuses on the capacity of political institutions to address the conflicting interests of women and men that produce gendered asymmetries in resource access and social opportunity. It examines the contrasting terms of women's engagement in politics in the two countries and the consequences these terms have for their perceived legitimacy as politicians, and for their capacity to promote gender equality in new legislation. The unprecedented numbers of women in politics in these countries offer an opportunity to identify conditions favouring women's political effectiveness. Ways of consolidating and institutionalizing gender-sensitive changes to accountability systems and institutions are considered.

KIT Library code P 03-723

057   Citizens as partners: OECD handbook on information, consultation and public participation in policy-making
GRAMBERGER, MARC. Organisation for Economic Co-operation and Development (OECD), Paris, 2001
This handbook is a practitioner's guide designed for use by government officials in OECD Member and non-member countries. It offers a practical 'road map' for building frameworks for informing, consulting and engaging citizens during policymaking. The handbook recognizes the great diversity of country contexts, objectives and measures in strengthening government-citizen relations. It offers no prescriptions or ready-made solutions, but it seeks to clarify the key issues and decisions faced by government officials when designing and implementing measures to ensure access to information, opportunities for consultation and public participation in policymaking in their respective countries. Policy lessons and examples are drawn from the OECD report entitled 'Citizens as partners: information, consultation and public participation in policymaking'. The report is the result of over two years of joint efforts by OECD Member countries and represents a unique source of comparative information on measures taken for strengthening citizens' access to information,

gender, citizenship and governance

consultation and participation in policymaking. A short Policy Brief designed for policymakers, setting out the report's main findings and policy lessons, is also available on the OECD website (www.oecd.org).

URL: http://www1.oecd.org/publications/e-book/4201141E.pdf

058   Electoral gender quotas: lessons from Argentina and Chile
GRAY, TRICIA JEAN. *Bulletin of Latin American Research* 22(2003)1, p. 52-78, 70 lit.refs ISSN 0261-3050
A comparative case study examined the role of electoral quotas for increasing women's representation in Argentina and Chile. The central hypothesis was that gender quotas in favourable electoral systems increase women's representation, and a corollary hypothesis was that more women in politics should also promote gender issues in public policy. Since the transition of their respective countries to democratic regimes, many Argentine and Chilean women still promote gender issues, such as gender quotas, but the different transitions have now shaped the opportunity and space for gender issues in politics. Against this background, an overview of research on electoral gender quotas and legislative behaviour was given followed by a discussion of issues such as electoral systems, the establishment of gender quota policies, and the electoral results of Argentina and Chile, respectively. It was concluded that while gender quotas can indeed be effective, nevertheless the types of electoral and quota systems are important defining conditions and improvements in gender issues are not always guaranteed.
KIT Library code C 2850-22(2003)1

059   A decade of democratization in Chile: the effects of women's political strategies
GRAY, TRICIA JEAN. UMI, Ann Arbor, MI, 2002, xii, 349 p. ill. bibliogr.: p. 331-349 Doctoral diss. Miami University, Oxford, OH, 2000.
The effectiveness of women's political strategies since the transition to democracy in Chile is examined based on a gender analysis of democratization literature. The literature on gender and political participation reveals disagreements regarding the best way to articulate and pursue gender interests. Thus, applying a gender analysis to traditional political studies is one measure of women's effectiveness in democratic politics. Furthermore, studies of women's formal participation and non-governmental participation indicate gender distinctions in both objectives and strategies, and there are various explanations of how women's

distinct gender participation influences democratic politics. Gender interests are distinguished as practical care issues, gender equity issues, and feminist issues in order to better analyze class and ideological divisions among women. In Chile, women have pursued three strategies of participation since the transition to democracy: in formal state politics, in non-governmental politics, and in both areas. Thus, the women's strategies have practiced an institutionalized political strategy, an autonomous strategy, and a dual strategy. This study is a comparative case study of those three strategies, based on a historical analysis of women in Chilean politics and on interview data from women in various arenas of contemporary Chilean politics. The effectiveness of each strategy is determined according their respective objectives and the subsequent success in achieving policy access and policy influence, that is, in assuming positions of leadership in the state or non-governmental organizations and in securing policy responses or organizational programmes to meet gender interests.
KIT Library code P 01-2901

060   Approaches to civic education: lessons learned
HANSEN, G. United States Agency for International Development (USAID), Washington, DC, 2002
Over the past decade, civic education has become a major component of USAID democracy programming. Civic education is assumed to contribute to the development of a more active and informed democratic citizenry. The Centre for Democracy and Governance of USAID has undertaken a study to measure the impact of both adult and school-based civic education programmes on participants' democratic behaviour and attitudes in the Dominican Republic, Poland and South Africa. The results of the study show that civic education contributes to significantly greater rates of participation among programme participants, especially at the local level. However, the programmes appear to have little effect on changing democratic values. The study also found that men tended to receive greater benefit from civic education than women and that civic education tended to reinforce gender disparities in the political realm. An important finding is that course design and quality of instruction are critical to the success of civic education programmes.
Recommendations and lessons for designing more effective programmes were made.
URL: http://www.usaid.gov/democracy/pdfs/pnacp331.pdf

061   Representation of women in governance in Singapore: trends and problems
HAQUE, M. SHAMSUL. *Asian Journal of Political Science* 8(2000)2, p. 59-8, ill., lit.refs in notes ISSN 0218-5377

The issue of women's representation in various domains of governance, including the legislature, cabinet, administrative agencies, and local organizations, in Asia, with special reference to Singapore, was explored. First, the contemporary global trends in gender-related issues in general were analyzed, including the various anti-discrimination laws and conventions since the 1950s, the different international institutions that address gender issues worldwide, and the number of international conferences that further the gender debate. Yet despite all these activities, progress has been slow: globally, women still only occupy 6% of top managerial positions, earn 30 to 40% less than their male peers for comparable work, and constitute over 60% of the world's poor. The situation in Singapore is not much better. It was argued that, in Singapore's case, the study of gender must transcend the relatively trivial but well-publicized events, such as the increase in the number of women motor bikers, female authors and award winners, and focus instead on the extent to which women's representation and participation has increased in the administrative sphere. The class dimension should also not be overlooked: globally, the dominant voice for female representation still belongs to women from the social and educated elite, while women from the less privileged classes are still not heard.
KIT Library code D 3512-8(2000)2

062   Transnational NGDOs and participatory forms of rights-based development: converging with the local politics of citizenship in Cameroon
HICKEY, SAM. *Journal of International Development* 14(2002)6, p. 841-857, 81 lit.refs ISSN 0954-1748

The 1990s witnessed the emergence of a transnational community of non-governmental development organizations (NGDOs), a community 'expressing shared values, languages and practices...from Orissa to Oxfordshire'. During this period, NGDOs generally assumed that 'it (citizenship) is to be strengthened by community participation and local empowerment', using participatory development as a means to achieve this. Yet, the transmission of participatory development by transnational NGDOs to local partners in developing countries has been heavily criticized lately, primarily because of an apparent failure to attain the essentially political goal of empowerment. The

problem is the duel tendency to depoliticize issues and strategies of participation, and to overlook the local and historical context of citizenship formation in developing countries. Using the results of field research carried out in autumn 1998 and spring 2000 in Cameroon, this article explores how a local social movement there has become increasingly engaged in partnerships with the transnational community of NGDOs and examines how one participatory intervention has engaged with ongoing processes of citizenship formation amongst this group. The case study reveals the ambiguous implications of this strategy, and concludes by framing the challenge for transnational NGDOs who might seek to overcome these problems by adopting a rights-based development approach.
KIT Library code E 3118-14(2002)6

063   Gender and budgets. Overview report
HOFBAUER BALMORI, HELENA. *BRIDGE Reports*. Institute of Development Studies (IDS), Brighton, 2003

While government budgets allocate resources in ways that perpetuate gender biases, budgets also offer the potential to transform gender inequalities. This report maps out why gender budget initiatives (GBIs) are needed, how and by whom they are implemented, what strategies can strengthen their impact, and presents recommendations towards achieving a gender-sensitive budget.
URL: http://www.ids.ac.uk/bridge/reports/CEP-Budgets report.pdf

064   Targeting women: gender perspectives in conflicts and peace building
HÖGLUND, ANNA T. *New Routes* 6(2001)3. Life & Peace Institute, Uppsala, 39 p. ill. lit.refs ISSN 0248-0200

This special issue on 'Women and Peace' provides various perspectives on the effects of wars and violence on women and women's contribution to the peace process, using examples from Southern Africa, Serbia, the Middle East and Somaliland. Some of the contributions are short versions of papers that have previously been published.
KIT Library code H 2253-6(2001)3

065   Strengthening economic and financial governance through gender responsive budgeting. UNIFEM-OECD-Nordic Council of Ministers-Belgium government high level conference, Egmont Palace, 16-17 October 2001: conference report
HOLVOET, NATHALIE

The practice of gender-responsive budgeting is relatively new but rapidly expanding. A clear-cut

gender, citizenship and governance

uniform model of gender-responsive budgeting does not yet exist. A high-level, international two-day conference on 'Strengthening economic and financial governance through gender responsive budgeting' held in Brussels, Belgium in October 2001 attracted ministers, parliamentarians, experts and high-level policymakers from 43 different countries. It aimed to take stock of past experiences and build a common understanding about approaches, concepts, tools and instruments. The highlights of the conference are presented, including the opening session speeches, agenda and speakers, short biographies of the speakers and chairs, an overview of country statements, list of conference papers and list of participants. Three sessions discussed: (1) the context and future challenges; (2) tools and approaches; and (3) lessons learned in practice. Lessons learned focus both on in-country practices and on the development of the methodology in terms of overall conceptual models, frameworks and tools. A conference communiqué was drawn up proposing a global vision for gender budget initiatives. It was fashioned to enlist reiteration of commitments made by most UN Member States to undertake a gender-sensitive budget analysis and to add a deadline date: 2015.
URL: http://www.dgic.be/en/topics/gender/unifem/gender_report_conf_oct01.pdf

066   Engendering the right to participate in decision-making: electoral quotas and women's leadership in Latin America
HTUN, MALA N.; JONES, MARK P. In: Gender and the politics of rights and democracy in Latin America ed. by Nikki Craske and Maxine Molyneux. Palgrave, Basingstoke, 2002, p. 32-56, ill. 28 lit.refs
By the year 2000, 12 Latin American countries had enacted national laws setting a minimum level of 20-40% for women's participation as candidates in national elections. The current trend, visible throughout Latin America, of using quota laws to boost women's participation in government is unprecedented in world history. Today, women occupy 13% of the seats in the lower houses of parliament in Latin America, ranking behind Northern Europe (at 39%) but on a par with the world average, including the USA (also at 13%). Why and how did Latin America opt for quotas over another policy mix? Have these quotas achieved the goals invested in them by women's movement activists? Two arguments were developed about the effects of quotas on the election of women and on gender-related policy outcomes. First, it was shown that the quota laws have only been mildly effective in increasing

women's presence in legislatures. Second, evidence showed that when quotas work, women's greater presence in politics serves to shift the terms of legislative debates. It was concluded that, with the exception of Argentina, quota laws have been a relatively painless way to pay lip service to women's rights without suffering the consequences. Finally, broad-based political alliances, not quotas, are what it takes to produce legislative action benefiting all women.
KIT Library code P 01-2713

067   Governance in Vanuatu
HUFFER, ELISE; MOLISA, GRACE MERA. *Pacific Economic Bulletin* 14(1999)1, p. 101-112, 44 lit.refs ISSN 0817-8038
Vanuatu is an ex-Franco-British condominium made up of 80 islands with a population of approximately 160,000. The instability of successive coalition governments and inappropriate behaviour of several politicians since Independence in1980 has led to a 'crisis in government'. The issue of governance in Vanuatu is discussed against the current climate of concern among influential aid donors who are anxious to promote growth in the Pacific region while ensuring that their (decreasing) development assistance is used more efficiently. The relevance of the governance agenda in Vanuatu is explored and the ni-Vanuatu people's attitudes towards it examined. The main areas of concern articulated by the ni-Vanuatu people are presented. Differences between 'custom' and 'politics' are analyzed, as are the importance of education, consultation and gender. It was concluded that the best practices of the diverse societies that make up Vanuatu should be studied further so that they can be incorporated into a body of a Vanuatu 'brand' of democracy and Vanuatu 'made' good governance.
KIT Library code E 3028-14(1999)1

068   Gender and citizenship: what does a rights framework offer women?
HUQ, SHIREEN P. *IDS Bulletin* 31(2000)4, p. 74-82, ill. ISSN 0265-5012
Feminists and women's organizations in different parts of the world have made creative use of the Convention on the Elimination of All Forms of Discrimination Against Women (CEDAW) and other international instruments to raise awareness around issues of social justice and equality. Naripokkho, an activist women's organization in Bangladesh, is one such group. Founded in 1983, Naripokkho focuses on two key issues: women's health and violence against women. Its approach is simple but effective: to 'create a voice that counts'; to 'demand answers';

and to 'demand change'. Many aspects of its work are discussed, such as its information gathering activities on the extent of violence against women; its successful negotiations with the Inspector General of Police resulting in a review of all cases of acid attack against women; how it convened a broad-based human rights alliance to resist the violation of sex workers rights as citizens; and its proactive role in the interpretation of the relevant reproductive health actions for Bangladesh. Its strategy in using international commitments to further its cause, particularly with regard to CEDAW, is explored in detail. Examples of its many successes, and failures, when seeking cooperation from the state or challenging the state's actions are given.
KIT Library code E 1978-31(2000)4

069   States of conflict: gender, violence and resistance
JACOBS, SUSIE; JACOBSON, RUTH; MARCHBANK, JEN. Zed, London, 2000, ix, 246 p. ill. lit.refs ISBN 1-85649-656-2
The relation between gender and violence at different levels and across national and social spaces is explored. In particular, the relation of conflict to state power and to state regimes is examined. While having a focus on gender, other social cleavages are also considered including race/ethnicity, agency and action, interwoven with the discussion of militarization. Among the issues addressed are: can national and international regimes offer women security; what is the meaning of women's recruitment to the military or their support for right-wing movements and regimes; and the importance of social cleavages other than gender in women's, and men's, experiences of violent conflict. Case studies from China, Brazil, India, Ireland and South Africa are included.
KIT Library code P 00-207

070   Advancing governance through peer learning and networking: lessons learned from grassroots women
JAECKEL, MONIKA. Huairou Commission, Brooklyn, NY, 2003
The last decade marks a growing interest of the development community in good governance as well as a growing awareness of the positive relation between female participation and good governance. Grass-roots women's groups deal with everyday survival issues and the social cohesion of their families and communities. In doing so, they develop ingenious solutions to issues like drinking water and sanitation, housing, health, and the eradication of poverty. They hold a valuable, first hand knowledge base

of what works and what does not work on the ground. To learn from this rich reservoir of expertise and to increase the influence of grass-roots women's perspectives on public policy, the Huairou Commission with the support of the LIFE Global Programme of IDG/BDP/UNDP launched the 'Our best practices campaign for local governance'. LIFE/UNDP promotes 'local-local' dialogue and action to improve the lives of the poor and influence policies related to participatory governance. This report is a reflection on the process, results and key lessons of the Huairou Commission campaign.
URL: http://www.iula-int.org/iula/upload/docs/ advancinggovernancethroughpeerlearningandnetworki g(huairou2003).pdf

071   Joint workshop on governance, poverty reduction and gender equality. United Nations (UN), Interagency Meeting on Women and Gender Equality (IAMWGE) and the OECD/DAC Working Party on Gender Equality (WP-GEN), 23-25 April 2001, Vienna
The workshop was held to examine interrelations between good governance, poverty reduction and gender equality as important dimensions of sustainable, people-centred and peaceful development. Conceptual and theoretical linkages between the three issues, as well as strategies and instruments for achieving the international development targets for good governance, poverty reduction, gender equality and the empowerment of women were discussed including sector-wide approaches, gender-responsive budgets and poverty reduction strategies. The roles of different actors such as governments, bilateral and multilateral donors, and civil society were looked at. Parallel discussions were held under two different tracks. Track 1 examined good governance, poverty reduction and gender equality in the context of broader development frameworks; track 2 discussed gender analysis, capacity building, and participatory methods as tools to support better governance results, reduce poverty and contribute to gender equality and empowerment of both women and men. Recommendations conclude the report.
URL: http://www.un.org/womenwatch/ianwge/ collaboration/viennafvjan2002.pdf

072   Gender and citizenship in the Middle East
JOSEPH, SUAD; KANDIYOTI, DENIZ. *Contemporary Issues in the Middle East.* Syracuse University Press, Syracuse, NY, 2000, xxxi, 400 p. bibliogr.: p. 347-380 ISBN 0-8156-2865-X

gender, citizenship and governance

The papers contained in this book illustrate the various ways in which women fall short of being vested with the rights and privileges that would define them as fully enfranchised citizens in the Middle East region. They comprise country studies from Egypt, Algeria, Tunisia, Morocco, Sudan, Lebanon, Palestine, Jordan, Iraq, Saudi Arabia, Yemen, Turkey, Iran and Israel. Many offer an in-depth examination of national legislation on personal status, penal law, labour law, nationality and social security law. Some include indicators such as female education and employment, and many comment on the types of mobilization and activism engaged in by Middle Eastern women themselves to press for an expansion of their citizenship rights.
KIT Library code P 01-160

073   Gender related problems of women, women's empowerment and Panchayati Raj
JOSEPH, NEENA. Himalaya, Mumbai, 2001, xi, 218 p. ill. lit.refs ISBN 81-7866-243-4
In India, as elsewhere, women face many problems that constrain their political participation in local bodies. It is argued that women are needed in the Panchayati Raj institutions (PRIs) to represent women and their needs and problems at local level. Provisions, including the reservation of seats for women in local bodies, have been included in the Panchayati Raj Act to solve some of the problems faced by women. Following a review of the history of women's political life in India, the representation of women in Panchayats in Kerala is discussed and a few case studies are presented to illustrate women's performance in Panchayats. Problems experienced by women leaders in PRIs and ways in which women can be empowered through PRIs are described. A detailed discussion of the issue of reservation of seats for women in local bodies and parliament concludes the book.
KIT Library code P 03-312

074   Citizenship and the boundaries of the acknowledged community: identity, affiliation and exclusion
KABEER, NAILA. IDS Working Paper 171. University of Sussex. Institute of Development Studies (IDS), Brighton, 2002, viii, 40 p. lit.refs ISSN 1353-6141 ISBN 1-85864-473-9
The focus is on the interaction of two different forms of membership and the rights and responsibilities associated with it: membership of the imagined community of the nation state; and membership of various acknowledged communities at the sub-national level. These different forms of citizen membership help to shape prevailing patterns of access and exclusion, both separately and in interaction with each other. Thus the paper takes a sociological approach to citizenship, focusing on its implications for the distribution of rights, resources and recognition, but within the politically constructed boundaries of the nation-state. Citizenship performs an allocative function within these boundaries in that it controls access to scarce resources. Struggles for inclusion within the circle of citizenship are consequently struggles over access to resources. Citizenship also affirms and legitimates 'social standing' within a society: struggles over its meaning and membership are consequently also struggles for social recognition. The paper aims to contribute to the development of a research agenda on the theme of 'inclusive citizenship', in particular the challenges it presents in the context of poorer countries of the South, particularly those in South Asia and sub-Saharan Africa.
KIT Library code D 3443-(2002)171

075   Women in Egyptian civil society: a critical review
KANDIL, AMANI. Al-Raida (2002)97/98, p. 30-37 ISSN 0259-9953
Women make up half of Egypt's population so it is essential to understand the extent of their participation in civil society, especially given Egypt's moves towards democratic transformation. The level of women's political participation has steadily dropped in the last two decades, with even fewer women bothering to vote. It was argued that illiteracy, economic constraints, repressive cultural practices, and women's own belief that public and political activities are 'male concerns' deter women from participating in civil society organizations. The government is trying to improve the situation of women in Egypt and is working to create a complementary relationship between the efforts of civil society organizations and public institutions in order to achieve gender equity. Against this background, the different ways in which Egyptian women interact with the emerging civil society organizations are identified and explored. Women are found to be poorly represented in civil society organizations, with few decision making roles. The leadership positions are almost always held by men, even in the older organizations where women's historical presence goes back to the 19th Century. A wider field study is therefore needed to identify why women's participation levels have dropped. Awareness raising via the media and education would help.
KIT Library code H 2381-(2002)97/98

076 Gender perspectives on peace and conflict studies
KARAMÉ, KARI H.; TRYGGESTAD, TORUNN L.; BERTINUSSEN, GUDRUN. Norwegian Institute of International Affairs, Oslo, 2000, 168 p. lit.refs ISBN 82-7002-153-9
The application of a gender perspective in the analysis of different stages of conflict has been limited. One of the main consequences of this is that women's experiences, knowledge and efforts to a large extent have been left out. The prevailing understanding of conflicts, conflict prevention and transitions from war to peace is therefore mainly based on male premises. This book focuses on women's roles and the resources they represent in situations of crisis and conflict, and the importance of unveiling these roles and resources in Lebanon, the USA, Israel and Africa. It presents ethnographic work on the social consequences of warfare, and analysis that deconstruct concepts such as security, war, peace and citizenship to expose the gendered underpinnings informing theory. The arenas subject to analysis include military institutions, frontlines of war, feminist protest movements and community initiatives. All chapters were presented as papers in a seminar series entitled 'Gender perspectives on peace and conflict studies' organized as a collaborative effort between the International Peace Research Institute (PRIO) and the Norwegian Institute of International Affairs (NUPI) during May 1999-May 2000.
KIT Library code N 03-473

077 Gender and economic empowerment: capacity building through advocacy skills and training
KINUTHIA-NJENGA, CECILIA. In: Demanding dignity: women confronting economic reform in Africa ed. by Dzodzi Tsikata and Joanna Kerr; with Cathy Blacklock and Jocelyne Laforce. The North-South Institute, Ottawa, 2000, p. 221-235, 19 lit.refs
A project was carried out in two sites in Kenya: the agriculturally rich district of Kiambu and the pastoralist Maasai district of Kajiado. It had four goals: (1) to find out why so few women participate in decision making bodies at the district and local levels; (2) to identify local policy concerns from the point of view of women; (3) to examine the district budget in relation to women's needs; and (4) to identify training needs for rural women to improve their economic and social status. Women's participation in Kajiado was found to be minimal, yet in Kiambu more than 20 women leaders are active in economic decision making structures. The key policy

concerns of Kajiado women were: marketing, adult literacy education, education for girls and transport, while in Kiambu the women were more concerned about water supply, representation, transport, beer sales, and membership in cooperatives. Four key lessons were learned during the course of the project: (1) district development planning and budgeting processes rarely address women's needs; (2) district officers are not aware of the importance of involving women in district level planning and budgeting; (3) women at the local level are well aware of their needs which they articulated clearly during workshops; and (4) women at the local level are willing and able to learn how they can participate in and influence decision making.
KIT Library code N 01-1593

078 Putting women in their place? Participation in Indian local governance
KUMAR MOHAPATRA, AJAYA. *Development and Gender in Brief* (2001)9, p. 2-3, ill. ISSN 1358-0612
This issue contains four articles on gender and participation in development practice. The lead article stresses the need to mainstream gender-aware and participatory approaches into development work to ensure that development is truly equitable. Two articles explore innovative ways of dealing with organizational resistance to gender equity and the conflicts of interests that arise during participatory processes. One is about women's participation in local government in India; the other focuses on the participatory approach of Redd Barna Uganda, one of the country programmes of the Norwegian Save the Children NGO. A further article included in the issue explores the incorporation of gender into the poverty reduction strategies advocated by the World Bank.
KIT Library code D 3654-(2001)9

079 Gender and political participation in Hong Kong
LEE, ELIZA W.Y. *Asian Journal of Women's Studies* 6(2000)3, p. 93-114, ill. 18 lit.refs ISSN 1225-9276
The state of gender equality in political participation in Hong Kong is assessed using data from a territory-wide survey in 1996. The scope of analysis is broadened to include public participation at the grass-roots level and forms of public participation that are non-political but many have political implications. Three major categories of public activity are studied: (1) community participation; (2) activism via social participation; and (3) formal political participation. The findings reveal a rather low

rate of public participation of both men and women who tend to be active in different types of social organizations. Women, however, are less active than men in formalized politics and there are persistent social biases regarding women's ability to serve as community and political leaders.

080   Democracy and the status of women in East Asia
LEE, ROSE J.; CLARK, CAL. Rienner, Boulder, CO, 2000, ix, 213 p. ill. bibliogr.: p. 193-206
ISBN 1-55587-888-1
The impact of democratization on women's status in East Asia is explored. The first set of papers deal with the question of whether democratization promotes women's empowerment, drawing on case studies of women's representation and the political activities of women's groups in Japan, South Korea, Taiwan and the Philippines. The effects of political activities on the status and quality of life enjoyed by women in East Asia is looked at in the second set of studies, including country studies from South Korea, China and Taiwan. Somewhat disparate pictures of whether democracy holds out hope for improving the status of women's status emerge from the papers. Legal reforms have only slightly softened many aspects of patriarchy. Women's groups have become active in most of the East Asian nations, but their success has been varied and dependent on political factors outside their control. Moreover, gaining legislative representation for women has been difficult and not particularly efficacious when it has been achieved. More broadly, the overarching culture and political economy of East Asia have many biases against women. However, democratization has given women new tools to improve their position. How effective these tools can be and how well they are used differs radically among the individual East Asian nations.

081   Social policy and women's citizenship in South Korea: participation of women in the labor market and the national pension scheme
LEE, SUNJU. *Asian Journal of Women's Studies* 8(2002)4, p. 7-26, ill. 29 lit.refs ISSN 1225-9276
The gendered nature of the South Korean welfare state and social citizenship issues for women, with regard to their pattern of labour market participation and the National Pension Scheme, were examined. Since the economic crisis in 1997, South Korea has reinforced the gendered welfare state by granting social citizenship rights attached to labour market status. This type of social policy largely neglects the interests and needs of women and hinders the growth of their social citizenship. It was argued that in order to develop full citizen rights for women, the caring work that is performed mainly by women in the private sphere should be recognized as an obligation as well as a right that constitutes citizenship. Unfortunately, attempts made by various women's movements over the years to have the Korean family master system abolished have met with strong resistance by the Confucians. It was concluded that women's participation in the political sphere was therefore vital as it would help to eliminate gender discriminatory legislation while strengthening their civil right to work.

082   Conceptualising and addressing the mental health impacts of gender roles in conflict and peacemaking
LESLIE, HELEN. *Development Bulletin* (2000)53, p. 65-69, ill. 24 lit.refs ISSN 1035-1132
A model of healing, drawn from recent fieldwork with women survivors of conflict in El Salvador and from literature on gender and development practice, is presented as a way of conceptualizing and addressing the mental health impacts of gender-related violence inflicted upon women in recent Melanesian conflicts. This model of healing recognizes the inherently disempowering effects of gender-related violence for women and draws on the theory of empowerment to aid women in the reconstruction of their shattered identities and societies.

083   Towards realistic strategies for women's political empowerment in Africa
LONGWE, SARA HLUPEKILE. *Gender and Development* 8(2000)3, p. 24-30, 4 lit.refs
ISSN 1355-2074
Politicians, the media and even development organisations have many explanations for the small number of women in government: women's low literacy levels, non-assertiveness, poor leadership skills, all of which suggest that the problem lies within women themselves. Similarly, the strategies adopted by NGOs and development agencies to support women's political empowerment also rest on two (wrong) assumptions: (1) that women's increased access to resources, especially education, will lead to their increased representation in political positions; and (2) that governments are genuinely committed to leading national programmes of action for women's advancement. All agencies

supporting women's empowerment must recognize the true obstacles women face in gaining political power (the inculcation and acceptance of gender discrimination at an early age, a 'dirty tricks' campaign against those women when they do seek public office, and sexual harassment and intimidation when they finally make it), and develop programme strategies to overcome them. In addition to focusing on the need to get women into government, NGOs could also usefully support women's organizations that are engaging in direct action: a key strategy which enables women to push for policy changes from outside government.

KIT Library code D 3030-8(2000)3

084   Local government associations: promoting gender equity

LUNDKVIST, HELEN. International Union of Local Authorities (IULA), The Hague, 1999
Local government associations (LGAs) can play an important role in promoting and developing gender equality at the local level. At the national level too, LGAs are strategically positioned to represent local government, be a platform for policymaking, exchange experiences and promote good practice. However, not all LGAs have the resources or know-how to exert this influence. An overview is provided here of the possible areas where an LGA can act to promote gender equality. Examples of concrete initiatives and support for LGAs are also highlighted, including resources produced by the IULA international task force on Women in Local Government. The focus is on how LGAs can work to promote gender equality in local government in terms of their local government members, national government and international organizations. Cases from Botswana, Ecuador, Sweden and Canada illustrate this. The way in which LGAs can work towards gender equality within their own organizations is also addressed, so that they can be seen to practice what they preach. Finally, a list offering initial 'ingredients' on where an LGA can start is provided.

URL: http://www.iula-acb.org/iula-acb/documents/sboek5_eng.pdf

085   Making government work for poor people: building state capability. Strategies for achieving the international development targets

Department for International Development (DFID), London, 2001
This strategy paper explores the key governance capabilities identified by the UK's DFID as being key to poverty reduction. The central message is that the quality of government is critical to the achievement of the International Development Targets that have been agreed by the entire UN membership over the past decade. The paper notes that where progress has been achieved towards the International Development Targets, it reflects a parallel improvement in the quality of government. Progress could be faster if governance focused on key capabilities and worked in partnership with the private sector and civil society. The contribution of the international development community could be more effective if it were better coordinated and took more account of the local social and political context. Some of the challenges to be faced in achieving the key capabilities are: how the state should manage the process of withdrawal from direct engagement in economic activities and develop a new regulatory role; how policymaking can be related more effectively to revenue and expenditure management; and how the quality of services for poor people can be improved through the reform of public services and partnership between state and the private sector. Priorities for DFID are suggested.

URL: http://www.grc-exchange.org/docs/TSP.pdf

086   Dissenting daughters? Gender politics and civil society in a militarized state

MAMA, AMINA. CODESRIA Bulletin (1999)3/4, p. 29-36, 39 lit.refs ISSN 0850-8712
The feminist theory of state maintains that states are gendered. In militarized states, such as Nigeria, the gender politics of the military consists of the wives of senior military men being encouraged to play highly publicized roles and arrogated the leadership of 60 million Nigerian women. How have gender discourses within civil society been shaped by militarism? Has civil society generated its own gender discourses, or has it merely complied with those issuing from the regime? What happens to state-driven women's movements when the state collapses, shrinks or becomes increasingly authoritarian. These, and other issues are explored in order to examine how civil society and women's movements have evolved in Nigeria. During the recent period of extended military rule (1983-1999), initially militant Nigerian women's organizations became more instrumentalist than oppositional, stretching the boundaries between pragmatism and opportunism. The majority of women's groups seem to collaborate with rather than challenge the military state. Amongst women's organizations and mainstream civil society alike complicity appears to prevail over opposition to the gender politics of militarism. The recent increase in women's political activism offers

romising possibilities because it is driven by a
vision of a demilitarized Nigeria in which women
merge as cleaner, wiser and better political
leaders.

KIT Library code A 2752-(1999)3/4

87   Gender and democracy in Nepal
MANANDHAR, LAXMI KESHARI;
BHATTACHAN, KRISHNA BAHADUR.
Tribhuvan University. Central Department of
Home Science. Women's Studies Programme,
Kathmandu, 2001, 230 p. ill. lit.refs
ISBN 99933-57-00-6
The papers contained in this volume on women
and gender issues in Nepal have been first
presented at workshops and seminars. The
papers of the workshop/seminar on 'Gender
issues in changing Nepalese society' address the
impact of the shift in the Nepalese economy from
agriculture to other sectors, such as industry and
services on rural people, women in particular,
and look at women's political participation. The
papers presented at the workshop on 'Creating
awareness of equal property rights, political
rights and other issues among women' address
women's lack of information about legal
provisions, women's property rights and low
level of participation in decision making. Papers
presented at the 'Gender equality and
democracy' workshop/seminar focus on the
economic, socio-cultural, political factors as well
as on discriminatory laws that are hindering
women to enjoy democracy as men are doing.
The report of a workshop on strategies focuses
on 6 specific areas: the League of Nepalese
women voters, positive discrimination, equal
property rights, violence against women, gender
sensitization training, and the role of the National
Research Centre on Women.
KIT Library code P 02-2039

**88   Entrenching democracy and good
governance through the empowerment of women**
MCFADDEN, PATRICIA. *Southern Africa*
2(1999)2, p. 55-58
It was argued that a relationship between the
notions of democracy, governance and women
has never existed and that, until recently, most of
the discourses about democracy and governance
around the world have been about what men
thought in relation to the control, distribution and
production of economic and political resources in
their respective societies. Civil society has
consistently excluded women and what they
know, confining most of them to the narrow
spaces of the family and household. These issues
are examined in the African context and the
struggles and challenges faced by African

women today outlined. It is concluded that
women need to find the courage to construct a
political ideology of their own.
KIT Library code A 2748-12(1999)2

**089   Raising women's voices for
peacebuilding: vision, impact, and limitations of
media technologies**
MCKAY, SUSAN; MAZURANA, DYAN.
International Alert, London, 2001, 92 p. ill. lit.refs
Women's use of information and communication
and media technologies to raise their voices in
peace and reconstruction processes is the focus
of this book. An array of women's peace building
projects throughout the world is presented,
illustrating the diversity of the projects, the
creativity, and range of sophistication. The
importance of women's media and resource
centres is stressed, as well as their potential for
promoting women's use of media technologies to
build peace. Several of these centres are
achieving these goals. The use of media
technologies to support collaboration with like-
minded women's organizations to build peace in
their regions is discussed, using initiatives from
the Balkans, Africa, Latin America, Asia and the
Pacific. An example is given of how South
Korean women use media technologies to
facilitate peace-building. Findings are analyzed,
conclusions are offered and policy
recommendations to increase and enhance
women's use of traditional, appropriate and
sophisticated media technologies to build peace
are made.
KIT Library code G 02-1

090   Women and the aftermath
MEINTJES, SHEILA. *Agenda* 43. Agenda,
Durban, 2000, 102 p. ill., lit.refs ISSN 1013-0950
Violation of women during war does not cease
when peace is made but continues in the
aftermath that follows. The problems of
demilitarization and why gender violence is
transferred to privatized spaces in the post-war
period were addressed in the conference 'The
aftermath: women in post-war construction'
which was held in 1999. Issues raised at that
conference are the focus of the articles contained
in this special issue. In addition to a short report
of the conference, issues for research and debate
on women and shifting gender identities in war
and the aftermath of war in Africa are addressed.
Case studies are presented of women who have
successfully used networks, customs and song to
make peace, and women who have fought wars of
liberation in various countries including Angola,
Sudan, South Africa, and Burundi.
KIT Library code H 2379-(2000)43

101

091   The budget: a quick look through a 'gender lens'
MENON-SEN, KALYANI; SEETA PRABHU, K.
Economic and Political Weekly 36(2001)14/15,
p. 1164-1169, ill. ISSN 0012-9976
India's financial budget for 2001-2002 is
examined. Its implications for women's
empowerment, especially in light of the Indian
government's prior enthusiastic promises to
empower women, are analyzed. Gaps between
government promises and the reality of the
budget are exposed. Changes in patterns of
allocations to various women-specific schemes as
well as to schemes of indirect benefit to women
are identified, especially regarding women in
special circumstances, the education sector,
children's welfare, and the health sector. This
preliminary analysis suggests that the standard
perception of women's roles continues to be as
mothers and caregivers, and has undergone little
change. Cuts to allocations for poverty alleviation
programmes and programmes that can
potentially alleviate women's burden of unpaid
domestic work reinforce this image and
demonstrate a basic insensitivity to women's
priorities and problems that is all the more
surprising in view of the publicity around
Women's Empowerment Year.

092   Learning citizenship
MERRIFIELD, JULIET. *IDS Working Paper* 158.
Institute of Development Studies (IDS), Brighton,
2002, vi, 37 p. lit.refs ISSN 1353-6141
ISBN 1-85864-425-9
This paper is a discussion of three main threads
of research and practice that are generally
pursued separately: on citizenship and what
active citizenship entails and requires; on adult
education for citizenship; and on learning. The
starting point is the renewed interest in
promoting citizenship in many parts of the world.
The second element in the discussion is the long
and diverse history of education for citizenship.
Some of the ways in which citizen attributes are
learned and developed are reviewed: through
socialization into political cultures, indirect
learning through participation in community
groups and social movements, and education for
democracy including both popular adult
education and civic education by the state and
formal institutions. The final strand of research
dealt with in the paper is on how people learn. In
the last 20 years in particular there have been
significant advances in understanding how the
brain works, and the dynamics of 'socially
situated' learning. We have a much better
understanding of the importance of the social

context for learning, the role of experience and
action, and how the brain manages knowledge.
Although this research has not directly addressed
citizenship learning, it could contribute efforts to
promote active citizenship. In a final section,
questions and challenges for education efforts to
promote active citizenship are posed.

093   The rise and fall of Fa'ezeh Hashemi: women in Iranian elections
MIR-HOSSEINI, ZIBA. *Middle East Report*
(2001)218, p. 8-11, ill. lit.refs in notes
ISSN 0899-2851
In the Islamic Republic of Iran both politics and
women's political activities are now radically
different compared to before the 1979 revolution
yet one fact remains constant: politics remains
the domain of men and the few women who do
enter the political arena tend to be related to
prominent men. When the reformists won a
landslide victory during the Majles elections in
2000, this brought them one step closer to the
arduous transition from a theocracy to
democracy, a process that will doubtless continue
for some time to come. The painful changes of
this time of transition were nowhere more
evident than in the case of Fa'ezeh Hashemi,
daughter of the then President Ali Akbar
Hashemi-Rafsanjani and darling of the
'reformists'. A promoter of women's sports and
advocate of women's rights, she saw herself as a
true 'modernist'. Conservatives constantly
criticized her 'Islamically incorrect' ways. In
1998, opponents of reform drew up a hit list of
150 intellectuals, describing their murder as a
'religious duty'. A series of brutal murders
ensued and the country was gripped by fear. This
culminated in a full-scale press war between the
reformists and the conservatives, with
Rafsanjani as the main subject. Despite
warnings, Fa'ezeh took her father's side and in so
doing committed political suicide. Her rise in the
elections of 1996 and fall in those of 2000 are
described and used to illustrate how far Iranian
society has moved in the intervening four years.

094   Women in leadership in Vietnam
MITCHELL, SUZETTE. In: Gender and
governance with contrib. by Rima Das
Pradhan...et al. *Development Bulletin* (2000)51,
p. 30-32, 7 lit.refs ISSN 1035-1132
Vietnam represents an interesting case study for
the issue of gender in governance. It is a country
with a strong modern history of women in
leadership positions and currently has the
highest percentage of women in parliament in

sia. The historical events which led to this achievement are explored. An investigation, from field perspective, into how gender is being ncouraged in governance, is also carried out. ffirmative action in favour of women is traced ight back to 1930 when the Vietnamese ommunist Party created the Women's mancipation Association (later renamed the ietnam Women's Union). Unlike some countries the West, where women are still fighting for sues such as child care provision, access to ducation and employment, and legalized bortion, women in Vietnam were given them as art of government policy. They did not have to esort to employing a mobilization strategy such s a 'women's movement'. It is concluded that ietnam is a country where women's needs are eing identified clearly and progress is being ade with full government support.

95   Citizenship, civil society and women in he Arab region

IOGHADAM, VALENTINE M. *Al-Raida* (2002) 7/98, p. 12-21, ill. 20 lit.refs ISSN 0259-9953
he problematic nature of women's citizenship ights in Arab societies stems from a variety of actors: the absence of secularism and pre-minence of Islamic religious laws which reduce omen's status to that of dependants whereby ey must ask permission of their father, husband r other male guardian to marry, seek mployment, start a business or travel; the eopatriarchal' role of the state; and the absence r underdevelopment of democratic institutions the region. Yet, in many Arab countries, the truggle for civil, political and social rights is led y women's organizations, comprising highly ducated women with employment experience nd international connections. The fact that these rganizations exist at all is a sign of important emographic changes, of women's increasing ccess to the public sphere, and of the gradual rocess of political liberalization in the region. he various ways in which Arab women have ontributed to civil society, despite being limited y financial and legal constraints, the threat of arassment and arrest, and opposition by onservative Islamic forces, are explored. This ontribution manifested itself in literature, eminist movements, political lobbying, and ooperating with human rights organizations and ransnational feminist networks such as DAWN)evelopment Alternatives with Women for a [ew Era). It is concluded that women's struggles re the central motor of the drive for citizenship nd civil society.

096   The feminist project in cyberspace and civil society

MOJAB, SHAHRZAD. *Convergence* 33(2000)1/2, p. 106-119, 9 lit.refs ISSN 0010-8146
'Civil society', now a 'hot topic' in the academic world, is in fact a nineteenth century concept that emerged from obscurity in the1990s, triggered by political upheavals in the former Soviet bloc. A feminist critique of the concept was presented and examined from a Western and Middle Eastern perspective: in the West the main centre of power has shifted from the state to the market, yet in many non-Western countries the state continues to dominate the market and civil society. The optimistic view of the Internet as an open, borderless world in which no one can monitor the free flow of information was challenged, and examples of state control given. Far from being neutral, cyberspace was presented as a site where the individual, the state, the market and social movements engage in very unequal competition for hegemony. Based on the experience of the International Kurdish Women's Studies Network, a critical assessment was made of the claim that the current communication revolution has changed the balance of forces in favour of civil society. It was argued that by recognizing the contradictions and limitations of the virtual spaces of civil society our ability to create alternative forms of knowledge and learning would be enhanced.

097   Gender justice, development, and rights

MOLYNEUX, MAXINE; RAZAVI, SHAHRA. *Oxford Studies in Democratization.* Oxford University Press for UNRISD, Oxford, 2002, xii, 492 p. lit.refs ISBN 0-19-925645-4
Recent years have seen a shift in the international development agenda in the direction of a greater emphasis on rights and democracy. While this has brought many positive changes in women's rights and political representation in much of the world, these advances were not matched by significant increases in social justice. The chapters in this book reflect on the ambivalent record and on the significance accorded in contemporary international development policy to rights and democracy. The question of how far liberal rights agendas, whether embodied in national or international legal instruments, have taken account of women's needs and interests is addressed. The gender implications of the tensions between orthodox macroeconomic agendas, social rights and the delivery of welfare are highlighted in case studies from Poland, Chile and India. They consider how women's

annotated bibliography

movements have positioned themselves in relation to states and social movements that claim democracy as a legitimizing principle. Case studies from Iran, Peru and, South Africa and Uganda examine the political arena and the constraints on women's representation in political parties and in national legislatures. With reference to studies from Malaysia, Mexico and Uganda, the tensions between universalism and multiculturalism are discussed.

KIT Library code U 03-21

098   Money matters: workshop materials on gender and government budgets
Gender Education and Training Network (GETNET), Cape Town, 2000, 250 p. ill. lit.refs
The South African Women's Budget Initiative (WBI) is a research and advocacy exercise. Its main role is to examine the impact of government budgets on women and men, boys and girls and different groups of women and men, boys and girls. Modules have been developed for workshops aimed at learning people to understand government budgeting, to analyze how policies and budgets impact on women, and to develop tools to ask questions about government budgets and equity. The materials presented here can be used in workshops that look at gender analysis of budgets, but also within workshops that focus on specific sectors, on lobbying, or on gender. There are 3 modules: (1) what is a budget; (2) ensuring equity; and (3) lobbying and advocacy. Each module has instructions for facilitators, activities and handouts.

KIT Library code G 00-66

099   Women's political participation in SADC
MORNA, C.L. International Institute for Democracy and Electoral Assistance (IDEA), Stockholm, 2001
The degree of representation of women in the Southern African Development Community (SADC) and the barriers to women's political participation are assessed. The single major barrier to women's participation in decision making remains the cultural and traditional stereotypes around the role of women. It is concluded that empowerment of women must be accompanied by nationwide and regionwide campaigns, but that some social change is also necessary. It is no coincidence that two out of the three countries with the highest proportion of women (South Africa and Mozambique) are countries that have a proportional representation electoral system, and in which the ruling parties have had quotas for women. Gender considerations need to be built into existing and

ongoing debates on electoral systems. In additio to work at the regional level, each SADC membe country should come up with a national plan for promoting women's equal and effective participation in decision making.

URL: http://www.idea.int/ideas_work/22_s_africa/ elections/7_womens_participation_pdf

100   Gender, conflict, and building sustainable peace: recent lessons from Latin America
MOSER, CAROLINE O.N.; CLARK, FIONA C.
Gender and Development 9(2001)3, p. 29-39, ill. lit.refs ISSN 1355-2074
Civil conflicts have ravaged Latin America for the last thirty years. Yet Latin American experiences of conflict and sustainable peace building lack any gender analysis of the impact of conflict and the peace negotiations that end i much to the detriment of all those affected. Wh do Colombian women and men, in particular, ha to learn from these experiences? In May 2000, a workshop entitled 'Latin American experiences of gender, conflict, and building sustainable peace' in Colombia brought together 170 representatives from civil society, government and international organizations. Personal accounts of gender in conflict were presented, highlighting issues such as forced displacemen women (ex-)combatants; women's organization and participation in peace; and the problem of justice and reconciliation. Twelve recommendations for interventions for gender, conflict and building sustainable peace that can out of a global Conference which preceded the workshop in 1999 were listed. The three priorit areas identified at the workshop were: (1) the lack of voice of afro-Colombian and indigenous women in the peace process; (2) ex-combatant women helping other female ex-combatants reintegrate into society; and (3) promoting mor unity between women's organizations in genera and Colombia in particular.

KIT Library code D 3030-10(2002)3

101   Victims, perpetrators or actors? Gender, armed conflict and political violence
MOSER, CAROLINE O.N.; CLARK, FIONA C.
Zed, London, 2001, xi, 243, p. ill. bibliogr.: p. 217-235 ISBN 1-85649-898-0
The gendered nature of armed conflict and political violence is analyzed to provide a broad understanding of the complex, changing roles and power relations between women and men, whether as victims, perpetrators or actors, during such circumstances. Currently, armed conflict and political violence are predominantl viewed as male domains, perpetrated by men

cting as soldiers, guerrillas, paramilitaries or eacemakers. The involvement of women has eceived far less attention, with a tendency to ortray a simplistic division of roles between en as aggressors and women as victims, articularly of sexual abuse. Consequently the endered causes, costs and consequences of iolent conflicts have been at best under-epresented and more often misrepresented. apers and case studies from Africa, Croatia, srael, Palestine, Northern Ireland, India, El alvador, Colombia and Guatemala address 4 key sues: men and women as both actors and ictims; the stages of conflict and implications or women and men; political, economic and ocial violence forming a continuum requiring ender analysis; and local community rganizations, run and managed by women, laying a key role throughout conflict situations nd reconciliation processes.

IT Library code P 01-954

02   Gender and decentralisation: promoting omen's participation in local councils. Case tudy: Lira District, Uganda
IUGISHA, MAUDE. United Nations Food and griculture Organisation (FAO), Rome, 2000 etween February to April 1997, just before local ouncil elections, a 'Gender and decentralization rogramme' was implemented in Lira District, orthern Uganda. Under the auspices of the rogramme two workshops were held in each of e 24 sub-counties of Lira District in order to reate community level awareness, among both en and women, on the need to support women in eir efforts to effectively participate in local overning bodies. Other issues discussed in the orkshops included: sharing domestic chores; omestic violence; women and leadership; bstacles preventing women from taking on eadership roles; solutions to women's constraints leadership; and improving campaign strategies or local council positions. A couple of years ter, a case study assessed the impact of this ensitization programme and highlighted the essons learned. It was concluded that although e programme was rated as being highly uccessful, there was no guarantee that the uccess could be sustained. Recommendations ere therefore made for short- and long-term ollow up plans.

RL: http://www.fao.org/DOCREP/003/ 6090E/X6090E00.htm

03   Apolitical versus political feminism: e dilemma of the women's movement in Kenya
IUIGAI, WANJIRU. In: Legitimate governance Africa: international and domestic legal

perspectives ed. by Edward Kofi Quashigah and Obiora Chinedu Okafor. Kluwer Law International, The Hague, 1999, p. 67-107, lit.refs in notes
The women's movement perceives the societal roles attributed to each gender as contradictory. It aims to inform women of the contradictions prevalent in society to enable them to initiate change. Hence, women's rights are political rights. Against this background, the political evolution of the Kenyan women's movement is described. The role of politics in the women's movement in Kenya is examined in detail with the intention of showing that politics should be an integral part of the women's rights discourse and that denial of this fact is harmful to the women's movement at the ideological and practical level. Reasons why contemporary conceptions of politics in the women's rights movement should be abandoned are given. The relevance of the political versus the apolitical stance in the women's movement is examined. It is concluded that it is deceptive, deflective and even derailing to subscribe to a dichotomy between the women's movement and politics. Women's rights are political issues, inasmuch as they challenge the distribution of power, particularly in Kenya which is and always has been a patriarchy. Finally, the dangers of the 'Queen Bee' phenomenon in this context are explored and a redefinition of the political ideology of feminism in Kenya is proposed.

KIT Library code N 99-878

104   Governing for equity: gender, citizenship and governance
MUKHOPADHYAY, MAITRAYEE. Royal Tropical Institute (KIT), Amsterdam, 2003, 133 p. lit.refs
The KIT Gender department of the Royal Tropical Institute (KIT) in Amsterdam, the Netherlands initiated a three-year programme entitled 'Gender, Citizenship and Governance'. The cornerstone of the programme was the action research projects with 16 organizations and NGOs in eight countries in South Asia and Southern Africa. In October 2002, the conference 'Governing for equity' was held to discuss the findings from the research projects, develop ways of working towards gender equitable governance and contribute to a shared vision of the future. This report provides a synthesis of the presentations and discussions of the conference under the following headings: global debates on gender, citizenship and governance; women's political participation; engendering governance institutions; claiming citizenship; and governing peace. A key issue emerging in each session throughout the conference was that

governance is about power and politics. A key finding is that poor rural and urban women have a tremendous desire to be part of the political processes, however, corrupt and undemocratic it may be. These women saw it as their right to participate, precisely because they thought they could democratize political structures, systems and practice.

KIT Library code G 03-66/G 03-67

105   Local government, decentralization and gender. Paper presented at the Caribbean conference on local government decentralization, June 25-28, 2002
MYERS, ROXANNE.
Despite playing a productive and valuable role in society as a whole, women's participation in Caribbean local authorities remains low and limited. National governments and local authorities are losing out by not tapping into women's skills and talents, especially in the area of voicing gender concerns. This situation will only change with a massive increase in gender awareness at every level of society throughout the region. Four questions are considered: (1) to what extent can women be involved in transforming the gender inequalities that currently eliminate them; (2) to what extent is male preponderance a barrier to female political participation; (3) how can gender programmes engage men as partners with women to ensure gender equality roles; and (4) to what extent is community development aided by female participation in decision making. An overview of gender disparities in the political arena and their causes is given. Positive examples of women changing local government are also presented, with particular reference to Guyana. Ways in which women could be groomed for their new political roles are suggested. It is concluded that the future development of Caribbean societies depends on courageous women being willing to stand against the political status quo and take the reins of local government.

URL: http://www.ndi.org/worldwide/lac/guyana/localgov_conf/materials/papers/gender.pdf

106   Women, peace and security: a policy audit. From the Beijing Platform for Action to UN Security Council Resolution 1325 and beyond: achievements and emerging challenges
NARAGHI-ANDERLINI, SANAM B.
International Alert, London, 2001
This report is part of a broader International Alert programme to develop an auditing framework through which the responses of the international community to women's needs in conflict and post-conflict situations, and support

for their peace-building efforts can be monitore enhanced and encouraged. It provides an initial overview of some international instruments and outlines achievements and challenges at the global level. The focus is on evaluating the implementation and monitoring of national and international commitments to gender-sensitive conflict and post-conflict reconstruction. Some women's organizations appear to have had considerable success as part of policymaking processes. This suggests that when given an opportunity to participate, women have the capacity to make significant contributions. Recommendations include the development of guidelines for ensuring gender-sensitivity in post-conflict rehabilitation programmes.

URL: http://www.international-alert.org/women/polaudit.pdf

107   Empowerment and governance throug information and communication technologies: women's perspective
NATH, VIKAS. *International Information and Library Review* 33(2001)4, p. 317-339, lit.refs in notes ISSN 1057-2317
Expectations are high when it comes to the opportunities that Information and Communication Technologies (ICT) can offer to women in developing countries. In this context, the avenues created by ICT-enabled networking processes for women in the areas of empowerment and governance are explored, along with the obstacles encountered when engendering these processes. It is argued that in the context of the knowledge sphere, the issues of gender equality, equity and empowerment of women are even more significant as women hav a strategic role in the incubation and transfer of critical knowledge which often forms the blue print of survival for communities to adapt and minimize their risk in adverse circumstances. Positive examples of ways in which ICT has helped women are given, such as the e-commere activities of the 'Rupununi Weaver's Society' in Guyana, the GrameenPhone company's activitie in Bangladesh, a Ukrainian telecentre project, and India's Gyandoot intranet project.

KIT Library code E 2186-33(2001)4

108   Rural women in Kenya and the legitimacy of human rights discourse and institutions
NYAMU, CELESTINE ITUMBI. In: Legitimate governance in Africa: international and domesti legal perspectives ed. by Edward Kofi Quashiga and Obiora Chinedu Okafor. Kluwer Law International, The Hague, 1999, p. 263-308, lit.refs in notes

ural women in sub-Saharan Africa are twice
removed from the international human rights
system, because of their sex and poverty. Such
women constitute the 'voiceless majority' whose
voice remains unheard at international fora. In
light of this, the following question is explored:
Does international human rights and governance
discourse serve any purpose in the efforts to
advance the cause of rural women in Kenya and
elsewhere in sub-Saharan Africa. It is argued
that while the human rights regime, particularly
as embodied in the UN Convention on the
Elimination of All Forms of Discrimination
against Women (CEDAW), adopts an equality or
non-discrimination framework, structural
differences in power and control of resources
mean that the concept of equality does not always
protect women sufficiently. Next, an analysis is
made of the mechanisms which the international
human rights system, particularly CEDAW and
the African Charter on Human and People's
Rights, have to offer for the actualization of the
rights guaranteed to women. It is recommended
that the perception of the human rights treaty
implementation procedures ought to shift away
from mere routine compliance by states to
genuine accountability and that the treaty
implementation process be marked by both
active, broad-based deliberation at the national
level and wider participation by individuals and
groups at international forums.

109   Promoting the participation of women in local governance and development: the case of Ghana

OFEI-ABOAGYE, ESTHER. *ECDPM Discussion Paper* 18. European Centre for Development Policy Management (ECDPM), Maastricht, 2000, 30 p. lit.refs
The recent wave of state decentralization programmes throughout Africa is impacting European development programmes. Donors now have to develop new instruments to pursue their development objectives in a context of transition. Against this background the gender dimension of decentralization is explored, particularly with regard to initiatives to promote women's participation in local governance and the role of European support in Ghana. Efforts to increase women's participation as councillors and to promote their involvement in decision making are examined. Interventions promoted through local governments to reduce poverty and promote socio-economic development targeted at women are presented. European support for these efforts comes from organizations such as the German Development Service (DED), the Friedrich Ebert Foundation (FES), the Holland-based Institute for Housing and Urban Development Studies, the British Department for International Development (DFID) and Save the Children (SC). The work of the local capacity building and coordinating Institute of Local Government Studies (ILGS) in this area, including European involvement in its activities, is also highlighted.

110   Gender analysis and interpretation of barriers to women's participation in Ghana's decentralised local government system

OHENE-KONADU, GIFTY. African Gender Institute, University of Cape Town, 2001
This paper is a contribution to the dialogue on the new approaches to promote popular participation among citizens in local government. It focuses on the gender dimension of decentralization and adopts a multi-dimensional gender analysis to debunk the notions that carry with them intrinsic assumptions that the devolution of power to the grass-roots level will bring power closer to all the people, including women, and thereby improve governance. Using the case of Ghana's local decentralized local government system, the necessary conditions for an effective participation of women in political decision making positions are explored. Three questions are addressed: (1) how does decentralization promotes women's participation; (2) what explains the low numbers and ineffectiveness of women in decision making levels in local government; and (3) in what ways can the gender barriers be removed. Two approaches to make local government more responsive to gender and women's concerns, and to enhance women's participation in government are suggested: building women's capacity to attain and perform in local government; and encouraging stakeholder institutions to provide appropriate support to women's concerns by targeting positive action, creating an enabling environment, and providing education and required resources.

111   Democratization and state feminism: gender politics in Africa and Latin America

OKEKE-IHEJIRIKA, PHILOMINA E.; FRANCESCHET, SUSAN. *Development and Change* 33(2002)3, p.439-466, 70 lit.refs
ISSN 0012-155X
The contrasting cases of Chile and Nigeria are used to highlight some factors that encourage the emergence of state feminism during processes of democratization. While both countries are clearly very different, a comparative exercise is deemed

worthwhile as they both went through processes of regime change, from authoritarian to (more or less) democratic regimes, as part of a broader global way of transitions to democracy. Findings suggest that three key factors shape the strategic options available to women: (1) the existence of a unified women's movement capable of making political demands, such as the National Coalition of Women for Democracy (CNMD) in Chile and the National Women's Union (NWC) in Nigeria; (2) existing patterns of gender relations, which influence women's access to arenas of political influence and power; and (3) the content of existing gender ideologies, and whether women can creatively deploy them to further their own interests. State feminism emerged in Chile out of the demands of a broad-based women's movement in a context of democratic transition that provided feminists with access to political institutions. In Nigeria, attempts at creating state feminism have consistently failed due to a political transition from military to civilian rule that has not provided feminists with access to political arenas of influence, and the absence of a powerful women's movement.

KIT Library code D 1323-33(2002)3

112   Domestic, regional, and international protection of Nigerian women against discrimination: constraints and possibilities
OKOME MOJUBAOLU, OLUFUNKE. *African Studies Quarterly* 6(2002)3
Questions concerning human rights and discrimination against women are looked at from a perspective that differs from the dominant view within the human rights literature. This perspective has an intrinsic Western bias and operates on the implicit assumption that international human rights have their origins in Western liberal thought. It is argued that all human societies have a conception of human rights, even though there are cultural differences. The focus of the paper is on the constraints and possibilities that shape the environment of Nigerian women and either enable them to surmount the problems arising from discrimination or limit their ability to do so. The central thesis is that discrimination against women takes different forms in different societies and historical epochs, thus requiring differential strategies in each place and time. Discrimination against women in Nigeria is analyzed by examining the quality and content of domestic constitutional, regional and international protection and guarantees and the extent to which these de jure guarantees may or may not necessarily reflect the de facto condition of women in Nigerian society. In addition, the

following questions are addressed: (1) in what ways have structures of inequality been created in Nigerian society and how do these structures affect women's role women in contemporary Nigeria; (2) how can concrete problems that have a direct bearing on women's role in society be conceptualized and contextualized; and (3) how compliance with existing law to be enhanced to generate practical results.

URL: http://web.africa.ufl.edu/asq/v6/v6i3a2.htm

113   Women, the state, and the travails of decentralizing the Nigerian federation
OKOME MOJUBAOLU, OLUFUNKE. *West Afri Review* 2(2000)1
Despite ambitious plans to de-racialize and decentralize power immediately following independence forty years ago, Nigeria still bear all the hallmarks of a despotic, colonial state, with most Nigerians being treat as subjects not citizens by a small, elite ruling group. In fact, many of the problems caused by the colonial experience persist, especially the lack of economic development. Consequently, the country is impoverished. It was argued that unt the rights of citizenship are extended to all Nigerians, particularly women, through decentralization that allows full participation in the political process, the state will remain remo from the people and will fail to reach its full potential. Focusing on southern Nigeria, the way in which women in particular have been deliberately and consciously excluded from the political arena in both the pre- and post-colonial eras was explored in detail. Issues such as the meaningfulness of decentralization and the implications of unequal access which is embedd in the state structure were also examined. It wa concluded that an alternative, progressive historical analysis must be undertaken to refocu discourses on gender and politics. Fortunately, a few scholars have taken up the gauntlet.

URL: http://www.westafricareview.com/war/vol2.1/okome.html

114   The role of women in peace building
ONSARIGO, BEATRICE. *African Century Publications Series* (2001)4, p. 234-241, lit.refs i notes
Ethnic and regional conflicts have become the daily the norm in Africa and have sucked the continent into a downward spiral of underdevelopment. Thirty-five per cent of the world's refugees (7.84 million people) now come from Africa and people are more likely to die from hunger and violence here than anywhere else. Yet Africa has the largest reserve of natur and material resources in the world. It is argue

hat if Africa is to experience successful peace, hen peace needs to be redefined as the absence f economic and social justice, rather than the bsence of conflict within and between states. In his context, the historical role of women as eace builders at both the family and community evel in Africa in general, and Kenya in articular, is explored. As poverty, poor ducation, and exclusion from politics have lways hindered women's peace building efforts, ecommendations to improve the above are uggested, such as eradicating the image of omen as subordinates and replacing it with one f them as stakeholders; making education free nd compulsory for all; and eradicating raditions, cultures and practices that iscriminate against the girl child.

IT Library code H 2783-(2001)4

15   Making good on commitments to rassroots women: NGOs and empowerment for omen in contemporary Zimbabwe
SIRIM, MARY JOHNSON. *Women's Studies nternational Forum* 24(2001)2, p. 167-180, 4 lit.refs ISSN 0277-5395

ince the late 1990s, Zimbabwe has been rrestling with the severest challenges since the ost independence period, including a massive ncrease in HIV/AIDS, a failed referendum on the ew Constitution, the seizure of white-owned arms and a major economic and political crisis. his has seriously eroded the status of poor and w-income black Zimbabwean women. Yet, espite this dire situation, two women's rganizations have emerged that offer some ope, specifically for poor and low-income omen in Zimbabwe, namely the Zimbabwe Vomen's Resource Centre and Network ZWRCN) founded in 1990, and the Musasa roject Trust, founded in1988. These groups have ttempted to address the strategic and human ights needs of grass-roots women in Zimbabwe, articularly through disseminating information bout the status of women, providing training bout gender issues and working against omestic violence. These organizations, coupled rith the UN's Fourth International Conference on Vomen and the NGO Forum on Women held in hina in 1995, have promoted the empowerment f grassroots women in Zimbabwe and have iven a 'voice' to women's concerns, despite the ack-pedalling of the Zimbabwean state. In this espect, they demonstrate the increasing trength of civil society and the future ossibilities for women's enhanced contributions their communities and to national evelopment.

IT Library code H 2452-24(2001)2

116   Women in Arab civil society: a case study from Sudan
OSMAN, AMIRA. *Al-Raida* (2002)97/98, p. 38-42, 13 lit.refs ISSN 0259-9953

Sudanese women's involvement in civil society is explored and their roles in public life investigated, particularly in the area of conflict resolution and peace reconstruction. In Sudan, the political and public service arenas are generally dominated by men and there are still no women at the ministerial or sub-ministerial level. It is argued that although Sudanese women have entered public life as active members of male-dominated civil society organizations, e.g. trade unions, many obstacles still prevent their full involvement in the development and peace process. Seven recommendations are made to improve the situation, including: more training for women leaders in conflict resolution, mediation and negotiations; women's civil society organizations should appeal to the international community to support democratization and the peace process in Sudan; and women's civil society organizations should mobilize marginalized women, for example displaced women, refugee women and poor women to ensure that all voices of oppressed women are heard.

KIT Library code H 2381-(2002)97/98

117   Without strong roots the tree won't grow: women's activism, gender roles, and civil society in Mexico
PALIER, JUDITH ANN. UMI, Ann Arbor, MI, 2002, viii, 157 p. Doctoral diss. University of New Mexico, Albuquerque, 2000. lit.refs

Women in Mexico, as elsewhere, engage in a broad range of activism directed at various goals. They may become empowered through their grass-roots activism, even when it is not directed at empowering women. The processes and mechanism through which women become empowered by their activism are the subject of this dissertation. The process of empowerment through activism depends upon the internal dynamics, decision making processes and communication patterns of activist groups. The origins of those dynamics, processes and patterns, and the effects they have on the survival of groups as well as empowerment of members, are looked at. Grass-roots activist groups offer the possibility of democratizing Mexico's authoritarian civil society, and of themselves providing new models of authority and new ways of doing politics. The potential of these autonomous, self-constituted groups to democratize Mexico's authoritarian political system is also examined. It is concluded that

grass-roots activist groups can function to democratize civil society, facilitating a transition to democracy in Mexico. However, democratization of Mexico's civil society is dependent upon the models of politics adopted by groups, and on the groups' ability to resist co-optation and determine the nature of their linkages to the state.
KIT Library code P 01-2752

118   Parliament and the budgetary process, including from a gender perspective. Regional seminar for English-speaking African parliaments, 22-24 May 2000, Nairobi (Kenya)
Reports and Documents 38. Inter-Parliamentary Union (IPU), Geneva, 2001, 96 p. ill. lit.refs ISBN 92-9142-083-2
The Nairobi regional seminar was organized to exchange views and experiences on the respective roles and functions of government and parliament in the budgetary process and paid special attention to ways in which a gender perspective in the budget may in fact highlight incomes that are usually 'invisible' or neglected. This publication is a recapitulation of what transpired during the Nairobi seminar. It contains the various speeches made at the inaugural ceremony, the texts of the presentations made by resource persons, the summary report of the proceedings by the President of the seminar, quotes from the debates, the Nairobi Declaration, adopted by consensus, and the key issues and guidelines which emerged from the seminar.
KIT Library code U 02-296

119   Rethinking participation, empowerment, and development from a gender perspective
PARPART, JANE L. In: Transforming development: foreign aid for a changing world ed. by Jim Freedman. University of Toronto Press, Toronto, 2000, p. 222-234
Participation and empowerment are the latest buzzwords, yet expectations of this approach vary. Mainstream development agencies tend to look to participation for increased efficiency and economic empowerment of the poor within the established structures of governance, while more alternative development stresses the role of participatory empowerment techniques in social transformation. Both groups find the participatory rural appraisal (PRA) approach useful. The apparent contradiction of such widespread popularity of PRA and participatory empowerment approaches is analyzed and the strengths and weaknesses of this approach, from the vantage point of women, explored. The PRA approach developed by Robert Chambers is examined in this context. It is concluded that PRA's successes are undoubted and important. However, the strong body of research carried o▪ on PRA since 1994 clearly warns us that gender inequalities will not disappear by giving voice t◾ women or simply including them in developmen▪ activities. The challenge lies in thinking up new ways about participation and empowerment, particularly for women, and to use theoretical tools to design new methods and techniques that will benefit women.
KIT Library code P 02-39

120   The impact of Senegal's decentralization on women in local governance
PATTERSON, AMY. *Canadian Journal of Africa◾ Studies* 36(2002)3, p. 490-529, 85 lit.refs ISSN 0008-3968
The impact of Senegal's decentralization programme on women, especially rural women, in local politics was examined. First, an investigation was carried out into women's numerical representation in decentralized government institutions and the factors that contribute to that representation. This was base on national election data from Senegal's 1996 local elections and a case study of the Ndoulo rural council illustrating how electoral rules an◾ party policies influence women's representatio◾ An examination was then carried out of the variables that limit the ability of female officia▪ to represent women's interests. Based on the expressed concerns of rural Senegalese women women's issues were defined as development programmes for women and children that promote economic opportunities, access to labour-saving technologies, education, and healt care. Interviews in Ndoulo village with rural council members, local party elites and female political leaders in 2000 revealed why women a▪ under-represented in local governance and the factors that make it difficult for elected female officials to represent the interests of women. Even with a female Prime Minister in 2001-2002, women's representation is not equal to men's representation. It was concluded that the only way of ensuring women's involvement in politics was to create new institutions and promote long-term cultural changes through education and by providing positive role models for female candidates.
KIT Library code A 2201-36(2002)3

121   Gender and conflict early warning: a framework for action
PIZA-LOPEZ, EUGENIA. International Alert, London, 2002

gender, citizenship and governance

here is an increased attention to the ctimization of women during wars, and a reater recognition of women's roles in conflict anagement and peace building. At the same me, early warning systems are playing a reater role in the international arena, in entifying areas at risk of violent conflict. Early arning analysis now increasingly concentrates n the grass-roots level, working with major akeholders and cooperating with local partners. owever, gender remains largely absent in the e-conflict context and early warning exercises, cluding the development of response options. A amework on how to 'engender' early warning at incorporates gender-sensitive indicators into formation collection and analysis is presented. ender analysis and perspectives should be ken into account in the formulation of response tions to ensure that discriminatory policies are t perpetuated in post-conflict situations, or new eedoms reversed. A list of gender-sensitive rly warning indicators is proposed and commendations for future research and action e made.

RL: http://www.international-alert.org/women/ gender.pdf

2   Progress of the world's women 2002. nder equality and the Millennium velopment Goals
ited Nations Development Fund for Women NIFEM), New York, NY, 2003
is second volume of the Progress of the World's omen 2002, a report of the United Nations Fund r Women, presents data and analysis related to al 3 of the Millennium Development Goals DG): 'promote gender equality and empower men'. An international cross-country sessment of women's situation at the beginning the new millennium, using the MDG indicators Goal 3 is presented. This information updates e review undertaken in 'Progress 2000'. fferent initiatives being undertaken in countries d regions worldwide to assess progress towards nder equality are highlighted. The report veals that although women have progressed atively slowly in the last two years in the areas education, literacy and employment, there have en encouraging signs of improvement in men's legislative representation. The increase women's share of seats in parliament was ributed mainly to political measures in several untries, where quotas were legislates or adopted a voluntary basis. Furthermore, the report veals that unlike other indicators of progress, ich show systematic differences between althy and poor countries and an undeniable link tween poverty and gender inequality, there are

no such differences in terms of women's participation in national governments. This is the only indicator that is not affected by national poverty, resulting in the fact that in some wealthy countries, women's political participation is well below that achieved in many developing countries.
URL: http://www.unifem.org/www/resources/ progressv2/index.html

123   The 'feminine paradox' in the tragedy of regional conflicts: the case of the Great Lakes region
PURUSI SADIKI, JEAN-JACQUES. *African Century Publications Series* (2001)4, p. 445-465, lit.refs in notes
A new phenomenon has gripped Central Africa: wars and massacres that target women and children. Since the wave of 'blind violence' unleashed in this sub-region in 1959 with the 'Hutu social revolution' in Rwanda, it has become common practice for military factions and local powers to launch brutal attacks against women and other vulnerable groups such as children, the elderly, and the disabled. It was against this background that the recent massacres of women and children in the Great Lakes region around the Omo valley in Central Africa were analyzed and placed in historical context. Wars have always existed in this part of Africa, but this is the first time that women and children have been the main targets. In order to gain insights into why this is happening, the role of women in preventing conflicts before colonization was explored with special reference to issues such as the blood pact, women in the Great Lakes monarchies, women in pre-colonial societies, women and political power in pre-colonial Africa, and women and colonial power. It is argued that the tragedies shaking the Great Lakes region have a name: mismanagement and the inadequate interpretation of the culture shock generated by tradition meeting modernity in Africa. Some ideas for a solution, from controlling to preventing conflicts, are suggested. These include efforts at the local level; remobilizing resources currently used to obtain weapons; installing a multinational peace-making force in the region; and setting up national, regional and international committees to oversee the application and implementation of the resolutions adopted.
KIT Library code H 2783-(2001)4

124   International perspectives on gender and democratisation
RAI, SHIRIN M. *Women's Studies at York*. Macmillan, Basingstoke, 2000, ix, 207 p. lit.refs
ISBN 0-333-75005-5

Some of the issues that women in different countries face during and through the process of democratization are explored in terms of four broad themes: (1) the importance of women's participation in political movements; (2) the importance of women's participation in processes of institution, constitutional and legal, design; (3) institutional practice at different levels, the national and international; and (4) the need for constant vigilance in any engagement with state-initiated and dominated processes of democratization. These themes are addressed in the experiences of women's democratic struggles from Mexico, Guatemala, Pakistan, the Arab world, Botswana, East Central Europe, Britain, India, South Africa and Australia. The emphasis is on the historical and political specificities of regions, movements and ideas and on the ways that women's movements assess their immediate and long-term interests. The nine case studies focus on women's struggles for a political presence in human rights, citizenship rights and democratic institutional entitlements to citizenship.

KIT Library code P 00-366

125   Leadership for social transformation: some ideas and questions on institutions and feminist leadership

RAO, ARUNA; KELLEHER, DAVID. *Gender and Development* 8(2000)3, p. 74-79, 12 lit.refs
ISSN 1355-2074
The challenge of the feminist movement is to change the rules, not play by them, however tempting. The institutions that rule our world were founded on a nineteenth century mixture of patriarchal beliefs, such as militarism and theories of social Darwinism. They are, by nature, anti-women and exclusionary. This article argues that institutions themselves need to be reformed, not the women working in them, so that they can reflect and promote gender equality. It describes how institutions in their current form block efforts to promote gender equality and suggests that recent efforts to professionalize NGOs have exacerbated this tendency. 'Organizational learning', on the other hand, could offer such institutions a 'third way: one that combines professionalism with feminist ideals, including the devolution of power. The article finishes with a discussion of the kind of leadership required to challenge institutional inequality, and suggests directions for learning.

KIT Library code D 3030-8(2000)3

126   Women in contemporary democratization

RAZAVI, SHAHRA. *Occasional Paper Geneva 2000: the Next Step in Social Development* 4. United Nations Research Institute for Social Development (UNRISD), Geneva, 2000, xiii, 45 ill. lit.refs ISBN 92-9085-024-8
Over the past two decades authoritarian regimes in many parts of the world have been replaced democracies. This paper looks at the issue of democratization from a gender perspective. Women's persistent exclusion from formal politics, in particular, raises a number of specifi questions about how to reform democratic institutions, since these institutions are not automatically gender-equitable. It is questioned whether affirmative action may not be dealing with symptoms rather than tackling the underlying causes. It is argued that women's groups and movements must engage with the political mainstream while remaining ever conscious of the risks of co-option by the state party in power. It is suggested that women have to simultaneously work at different levels both inside and outside the mainstream, forge strategic insider-outsider alliances, and to remember that the success of Nordic electoral engineering initiatives was made possible by th social democratic tradition.

KIT Library code K 3051-(2000)4

127   Gender and budgets. Supporting resources collection

REEVES, HAZEL; SEVER, CHARLIE. *BRIDGE Reports.* Institute of Development Studies (IDS Brighton, 2003
While government budgets allocate resources i ways that perpetuate gender biases, budgets al offer the potential to transform gender inequalities. This report on gender and budgets presents a supporting resources collection that features summaries of key materials, including case studies, tools, guidelines and training materials, web resources and networking contacts.

URL: http://www.ids.ac.uk/bridge/reports/CEP-Budge SRC.pdf

128   Women, war and peace: the independent experts' assessment on the impact of armed conflict on women and women's role i peace building

REHN, ELISABETH; JOHNSON SIRLEAF, ELLEN. United Nations Development Fund for Women (UNIFEM), New York, NY, 2002
Conflict can change traditional gender roles; women may acquire more mobility, resources, and opportunities for leadership. However, the

dditional responsibility comes without any
iminution in the demands of their traditional
oles. Women and men experience the conflict
ifferently; women rarely have the same
esources, political rights, authority or control
ver their environment and needs that men do. In
ddition, their caretaking responsibilities limit
heir mobility and ability to protect themselves.
lumanitarian assistance has failed to address
ne causes and consequences of women's
ictimization (discrimination, violence, and
narginalization). Women continue to have the
east access to protection and assistance
rovided by the state or international
rganizations. This report documents and
nalyzes the specific impact of war on women
nd the potential of bringing women into peace
rocesses. It addresses ten central themes:
iolence against women; displacement; health;
IIV/AIDS; organizing for peace; peace
perations; justice and accountability; media and
ommunications; reconstruction; and prevention.
ey recommendations to protect and empower
omen are made.
RL: http://www.unifem.undp.org/resources/
ssessment/index.html

29   'Put your money where your mouth is!'
he need for public investment in women's
rganisations
IORDAN, SIOBHAN. *Gender and Development*
(2000)1, p. 63-70, 47 lit.refs ISSN 1355-2074
he scope and range of women's organizations
round the world at the start of the twenty-first
entury is an impressive testimony to women's
rganizing efforts and demonstrates the
iversity of women's agendas. Yet despite their
uccess, a lack of adequate funding hampers the
apacity of women's organizations in the United
Kingdom and elsewhere to influence and shape
olitical and economic agendas. Why is it then
hat so many women's organizations in the UK
xist on the margins of viability, with dilapidated
ffices, out-of-date equipment, poorly paid staff,
nd inadequate funds? This question prompted a
esearch study (1996-1999) into the whole issue of
ublic investment in women's organizations. It
vas found that women's organizations which aim
o empower women remain largely unsupported
oth by national governments and bilateral aid
gencies. It was concluded that if political
hetoric about women's equality, be it at a local,
egional, national or international level, is to
ecome a reality, then investment of public
esources is necessary and should be monitored.
IT Library code D 3030-8(2000)1

130   Islam, democracy and the status of
women: the case of Kuwait
RIZZO, HELEN MARY. UMI, Ann Arbor, MI,
2002, x, 151 p. ill., bibliogr.: p. 138-151 Doctoral
diss. Ohio State University, Columbus, 2000.
Women in Kuwait are excluded from basic
political rights such as voting and running for
parliament. By examining organizations that
vary along religious interpretations, status lines
and organizational goals, the effects of Islamic
beliefs and practices and perceptions of their
social position on political participation and
support for women's rights are studied. Leaders
of women's organizations were interviewed and
members of these organizations were surveyed
to examine the relationship between Islam,
status, and political participation. It is found that
there is a differentiation between the
associations according to their leaders. The
leaders of professional associations goals to
improving women's place in politics and society
more often and more forcefully than did leaders
of the more numerous service organizations,
while the service organizations were more
concerned with encouraging Islamic lifestyles
and charitable works among their members.
However, the member survey reveals that the
members who support women's rights have
resources which gives the struggle for political
rights in Kuwait a reason to be optimistic. There
is a core of educated, religious, organized and
politically active women. These women see the
inequality in the political system and are working
towards achieving women's rights.
KIT Library code P 01-349

131   Decentralization measures and gender
equalities: experiences in Uganda
SAITO, FUMIHIKO. *Ryukoku Journal of
Economic Studies* 41(2002)5
Decentralization has been pursued in many
developing countries since the late 1980s in the
firm belief that this will lead to more efficient
public administration, more effective
development and all-round 'good governance'.
Between 1998 to 2000, fieldwork was carried out
in Uganda to examine how its decentralization
efforts have affected one of the most significant
disadvantaged social groups: women. The
Ugandan case is unique for three reasons: (1) the
structural reforms carried out since 1986 were
not 'donor driven'; (2) an 'indigenous' African
democracy is being pursued in the country; and
(3) the local council (LC) system, set up a decade
ago, also serves as an effective mechanism for
development in Uganda, not just a tool for
political democratization. Affirmative measures
taken by the current administration of the

National Resistance Movement (NRM) to address gender inequities are outlined, along with its reasons for doing so. The way in which women interact with the LCs and the impact of some donor agency gender programmes on rural women in Uganda are explored. It is concluded that men and women still have different views on respective roles therefore, in order to improve mutual understanding, a long-term learning process is essential: a process in which the lower level LCs could play a key role.

URL: http://www.world.ryukoku.ac.jp/~fumisait/en/gender.pdf

132 Gender-responsive government budgeting

SARRAF, FERIDOUN. *IMF Working Paper* 83. International Monetary Fund (IMF), Washington, DC, 2003

The concept of gender-responsive government budgeting (GRGB) and the extent of its implementation by national governments in both advanced and developing countries are examined. It is argued that in order for GRGB to be fully effective, obstacles such as gender-biased culture, the lack of appropriate budget classifications and the lack of gender analysis expertise and gender-disaggregated data in most countries need to be addressed. It is found that implementation of GRGB in a given country is not related to its wealth or technological status, but to the degree of the will or, more importantly, the size of the government's involvement in economic and social activities. Another finding is that while in OECD (Organisation for Economic Co-operation and Development) countries, women's organizations, NGOs, political parties and national or local governments have been influential in implementing the GRGB initiative, in developing countries (apart from some local NGOs and academia that have been promoting GRGB) mostly multilateral organizations and the donor community have been requesting and encouraging such an approach.

URL: http://www.imf.org/external/pubs/ft/wp/2003/wp0383.pdf

133 Engendering the new social citizenship in Chile: NGO's and social provisioning under neo-liberalism

SCHILD, VERONICA. In: Gender justice, development, and rights ed. by Maxime Molyneux and Shahra Razavi. Oxford University Press for UNRISD, Oxford, 2002, p. 170-203, 81 lit.refs.

The implications of the decade-long experience of NGO participation in social provisioning in Chile for the advancement of gender justice are examined. It is suggested that there is a fundamental contradiction between the rights-based agenda of present social democratic programmes and the requirements and limitations of a globalized economy and their negative effects on the lives of the majority of people. For feminists in particular, the experience of NGO participation in social provisioning of the last decade poses a serious challenge: are the present efforts to integrate certain categories of women, that is, the poorest of the poor, into the development process an advancement in women's rights? The social development strategy pursued by the two Concertación governments since 1990 in the name of 'growth with equity' is reviewed, focusing on the innovative social programmes implemented through a partnership between NGOs and governmental agencies. The gendered impact on people's working lives and communities from the processes and effects of intensified global economic integration are discussed in detail and it is argued that these social programmes fail to address these impacts. An outline is given of the implications of a gender equity agenda that aims to integrate women fully as subjects of rights into the development process but which does so by relying on the volunteer-like work of women, and which targets only those who are the poorest of the poor in a context of increasing, generalized social vulnerability

KIT Library code U 03-21

134 Power and representation: reservation for women in India

SHARMA, KUMUD. *Asian Journal of Women's Studies* 6(2000)1, p. 47-87, 43 lit.refs
ISSN 1225-9276

Recent developments is feminist politics in India indicate a growing concern with under-representation of women in elected and decision making bodies, and with the view that some form of reservation or affirmative action is needed to redress existing gender imbalances. The understanding of affirmative action or, in the case of India, reservation, includes notions such as equality of opportunity, social justice, positive or protective discrimination, compensatory discrimination, etc. Arguments for reservation have been advanced because gender balanced representation is expected to alter development priorities, perspectives and concerns. The current demand for parliamentary representation of women is built around several arguments and equal opportunity for participation in decision making is one of them. Women's interests and priorities are said to be

eglected in a male-dominated parliament and women's presence is expected to make a qualitative difference in increasing the empathy or their concerns. These arguments are countered by those who do not see women as a collectivity or who consider it is not only women who can best represent women's interests. Linking reservation questions to equal opportunity and social justice for women as a disadvantaged group has given rise to an inconclusive debate on the criteria for determining backwardness. Does it open the door to equal opportunity, does it realize social justice, and does it alter power relations. Many of these dilemmas apparent in the reservation debate have profound implications for political theory and practice and for the attempts by the women's movement to give a new meaning and dimension to the slogan 'political empowerment of women'.
KIT Library code H 2260-6(2000)1

35   New Panchayati raj: a functional analysis
SINGH, RAJ. Anmol, New Delhi, 2000, xvi, 259 p. it.refs ISBN 81-261-0628-X
The functioning of the new Panchayati Raj institutions after the Constitutional Amendment Act of 1992 in India is the focus of the papers. Five major themes are addressed: (1) women's participation in the Panchayati Raj institutions and problems encountered by women in discharging their constitutional obligation; (2) capacity building in Panchayati Raj institutions, in particular the knowledge and training needs of functionaries at the grass-roots level; (3) problems encountered by women's representatives of the Panchayati Raj institutions in discharging their roles; (4) perception of voters towards women's empowerment, participation and problems; and (5) decentralization of power at the grass-roots levels, participatory development and the Gandhian perspective of Panchayati Raj institutions. Together the papers provide an understanding of the functioning of new Panchayati Raj institutions in the post constitutional amendment era.
KIT Library code P 02-1064

36   Women in Indian politics empowerment of women through political participation)
SINHA, NIROJ. Gyan, New Delhi, 2000, 302 p. ill. it.refs ISBN 81-212-0686-3
Women's movements in India have been struggling for women's political empowerment for nearly five to six decades, yet women have only managed to get their demands for

quota/reservation in parliament and state legislatures included in election manifestoes of the political parties in 1991, 1996 and 1998 general elections. Constraints to women's participation in formal political institutions and process in various parts of India are examined within the context of gender and patriarchy. Analysis of women's role in the national freedom struggle shows that gender equality has never been the concern of the reformers in the late nineteenth century or the political leaders of the movement. The political participation of women has been severely restricted by gender and patriarchal norms that have perpetuated the subordination of women in the family and extended their subordination in the wider society, economy and politics. Adequate representation in representative bodies is very important for women's empowerment in the political process, and reservation and affirmative action is seen as the most potent strategy.
KIT Library code P 01-712

137   Gender, peace and conflict
SKJELSBAEK, INGER; SMITH, DAN. Sage, London, 2001, x, 228 p. bibliogr.: p. 207-219 ISBN 0-7619-6853-9
The key role of gender in peace research, conflict resolution and international politics is explored in this book that combines theoretical papers and case studies from Colombia, Yugoslavia and Sri Lanka to demonstrate the importance of a gender perspective to both theory and practice in conflict resolution and peace research. The theoretical chapters look at the gender relationship and engage with the many stereotypical elisions and dichotomies that dominate and distort the issue, such as the polarized pairs of femininity and peace versus masculinity and war. Drawing on examples from South America, South Asia and Europe, including former Yugoslavia, the case study chapters focus on issues such as sexual violence in war, the role of women in military groups and peace-keeping operations, and the impact of a critical mass of women in political decision making. The contributions are based on papers presented at an Expert Group Meeting organized jointly by the United Nations Division for the Advancement of Women (DAW) and the International Peace Research Institute, Oslo (PRIO) at the United Nations Research and Training Institute for the Advancement of Women (INSTRAW) in Santo Domingo in 1996.
KIT Library code N 02-90

138   Gender politics and policy process in Mexico, 1968-2000: symbolic gains for women in an emerging democracy
STEVENSON, LINDA S. UMI, Ann Arbor, MI, 2000, xvii, 369 p. ill., bibliogr.: p. 340-369 Doctoral diss. University of Pittsburgh, 2000
Women's participation and policymaking with democratizing processes in Latin America's emerging democracies is analyzed. It is hypothesized that in order for women to get their political demands met and policy advances implemented, they need to participate in higher numbers in legislatures, while at the same time continue to work across party, organizational, insider/outsider lines to build support for their interests. However, if their issues challenge socio-cultural or religious societal values, they will have less success. A political and policy process model is developed to test the hypotheses, using five gendered policy issues in Mexico over the time period 1968-2000: sex crime reforms; affirmative action quotas for women on electoral lists; sexual harassment; discrimination against pregnant workers; and decriminalization of abortion. It appears that multiple forms of women's participation are most effective in policymaking and overseeing implementation and overall women's efforts in these five issue areas have resulted in symbolic gains. The comparison of the political and policy processes indicate that changes in procedural democracy are necessary for change for women, but not sufficient for making transformative democratic changes.
KIT Library code P 01-2869

139   Strategies adapted by civil society and gender groups in integrating civil society and gender perspectives in the poverty reduction strategy paper (PRSP) in Tanzania
Ulingo wa jinsia 6(2001)3, p. 5-8 ISSN 0856-5805
Since 1999, the Tanzanian government has been developing a Poverty Reduction Strategy Paper (PRSP) in an effort to qualify for debt relief under the Heavily Indebted Poor Countries (HIPC) initiative. However, its approach has generated a lot of criticism from different civil society groups, including the media, who suspected that civil society and gender interpretations were not being effectively integrated into the document. These concerns prompted a number of initiatives, such as the Tanzania Coalition for Debt and Development (TCDD) and the Gender Mainstreaming Working Group on Macro-Policy. The goals, activities and achievements of these coalitions are outlined, including the recommendations made for inclusion in the strategy paper. Ultimately, the

government left the recommendations out of the strategy paper, claiming that it was too late to incorporate them but promising to consider them at the implementation stage. It is argued that if this position continues to be adopted by the government in future poverty reduction initiatives, the majority of women in Tanzania will continue to remain the poorest of the poor. For this reason it is important that NGOs and gender groups work together to advocate for these commitments to be honoured.
KIT Library code H 2691-6(2001)3

140   Women and leadership
SWEETMAN, CAROLINE. *Focus on Gender*. Oxfam, Oxford, 2000, 86 p. lit.refs
ISBN 0-85598-452-X
Despite the advances towards recognition of women's political, economic and social equality with men during the twentieth century, there is continuing lack of women leaders to determine the political, economic and social progress of humanity. Women remain absent from the key political and economic institutions shaping access to and control over resources. This issue is about leadership in many contexts: women resisting exploitation in the workplace; women heading households; women leading in the international policy forum. It offers insights for development policymakers and practitioners aiming to promote gender equality and to support women would-be leaders, and argues that the institutions that rule our societies themselves need to be transformed in order to promote gender equality. Countries featured include Bangladesh, Botswana, Guatemala and Uganda.
KIT Library code N 02-929

141   Gender implications for opening up political parties in Uganda
TAMALE, SYLVIA. Women of Uganda Network (WOUGNET), Kampala
For the last 20 years, Uganda has operated under a 'no party' political structure known as the movement system: a system that favours individual merit rather than party affiliation and which tries to accommodate all citizens regardless of their political inclination, tribe/ethnicity, religion or sex. Political indicators in Uganda point to an impending opening up of political parties that will allow for the uninhibited operation of parties that are free to compete for state power. Is this good news or bad news for Ugandan women? Will pluralism translate into better governance or into more democratic institutions? Will it help to close the gender equality gap that presently exists in all spheres of our society? While women have

gender, citizenship and governance

ndoubtedly made progress thanks to the
ffirmative action taken by the current National
Resistance Movement (NRM) administration,
evertheless it was argued that the Ugandan
tate (whether under Museveni's NRM system or
bote's pluralist system) primarily acted in the
nterests of self-preservation as a patriarchal
nstitution. Men still firmly hold the reigns of
ower and authority in Uganda, while women are
n power, but have none. Moreover, the state has
ven tried to roll back the clock on women's
ights on issues such as family land rights. It was
oncluded that the political space owned by the
JRM is deeply masculinist, anti-women and
ilitaristic and that women would be better
mployed if they distanced themselves from the
tate, increased their autonomy and focused on
he real issues that keep them in a subordinate
osition.
RL: http://www.wougnet.org/Documents/g
nder_politicalparties.html

42   'Point of order, Mr Speaker': African
omen claiming their space in parliament
AMALE, SYLVIA. *Gender and Development*
(2000)3, p. 8-15, 20 lit.refs ISSN 1355-2074
Vomen in Africa still represent a very small
inority of state national legislators: At the close
f the millennium, women accounted for ten per
ent or more of parliamentarians in only 17
frican countries. Yet politically active women in
frica have recently started to smash through
he gendered 'glass ceiling' in a bid to overcome
he cultural and structural barriers impeding
heir political careers. It is against this
ackground that the relationship of African
omen to parliament is examined, based on
terviews conducted between 1995 and 1998
ith 40 women and 15 male legislators in
Jganda's National Assembly as part of a
esearch study. Beginning with women's
volvement in politics in pre-colonial Africa, the
aper goes on to explore the barriers to women's
olitical activity caused by colonialism. This
istory explains much about women's absence
rom contemporary African national assemblies.
he case of Uganda is examined in detail,
articularly the policy of affirmative action and
he reality of male bias, prejudice, and day-to-day
exual harassment that women MPs confront
hen they manage to enter parliament. It is
oncluded that the struggle for women's
mancipation in African politics will be difficult.
t will take public education and awareness-
aising, equal numbers of men and women in
ational politics, and the radical transformation
f existing political structures.
IT Library code D 3030-8(2000)3

**143   Towards legitimate governance in
Africa: the case of affirmative action and
parliamentary politics in Uganda**
TAMALE, SYLVIA. In: Legitimate governance in
Africa: international and domestic legal
perspectives ed. by Edward Kofi Quashigah and
Obiora Chinedu Okafor. Kluwer Law
International, The Hague, 1999, p. 235-261,
lit.refs in notes
'When the composition of decision making
assemblies is so markedly at odds with the
gender...make-up of the society they represent,
this is clear evidence that certain voices are
being silenced and suppressed'. This premise
formed the basis of a study of the affirmative
action policies of the National Resistance
Movement (NRM) in Uganda since they took
power in 1986. Since then, the numbers of elected
women in Uganda has increased twenty-five fold.
Three categories of women were focused on:
members of the fifth interim legislature know as
the National Resistance Council (NRC); delegates
to the Constituent Assembly (CA); and members
of parliament (MPs) elected to the sixth
parliament in June 1996. Field notes from
observations in the National Assembly and
transcripts from interviews with 40 female and
15 male legislators formed the primary data set.
Following a general overview of the principle of
affirmative action, the issue of gender in Uganda
within the larger context of patriarchy and
underdevelopment is examined, especially as it
relates to the politics of parliamentary
representation and good governance. The
question of 'whose interests do female MPs
represent' is also explored in detail. It is
concluded that the pressure must be maintained
and that the women's movement must be ever-
vigilant against measures that substantively
undermine the gains that have thus far been
made.
KIT Library code N 99-878

**144   Technical assistance (cofinanced by the
Canadian international development agency and
the Japan special fund) for gender and
governance issues in local government**
Asian Development Bank, Manila, 2001, 22 p. ill.
lit.refs
This regional technical assistance (TA) addresses
the related issues of governance and gender in
the context of local government. Primarily the
TA aims to build the capacity of grass-roots level
women leaders in local governments to perform
their role and function more effectively and to
promote more efficient and transparent public
service delivery. The overall goal of the TA is to
promote and facilitate the linkages among

annotated bibliography

gender, poverty reduction, and good governance in local government, and to identify regional gender and governance issues for policymakers. The TA is being implemented in Bangladesh, Nepal and Pakistan. This document describes the background and rationale, objectives, scope, costs and implementation arrangements of the TA.

KIT Library code Br U 01-362

145   Gender and decentralization programme, Lira District, Uganda. Presentation to the second international meeting 'La parole aux femmes' organised by CESAO, 13-18 March 2000, Bobo Dioulasso, Burkina Faso, based on a case study prepared by Maude Mugisha
TEMPELMAN, D.E.
Community discussions on gender and women's participation in local leadership under the auspices of the highly successful 'Gender and decentralisation programme' implemented in Lira District, Uganda, from February to April 1997, produced interesting findings. During a workshop to explore men and women's perceptions about why women work more than men, men and women gave very different answers. Obstacles currently preventing women from taking on leadership roles included the fact that: men do not allow their wives to attend meetings fearing they might meet other men; a woman's heavy workload prevents her from taking part effectively; both men and women lack respect for women leaders; meetings are far away and therefore hard for women to attend; women have low levels of education; and women are generally shy, lack confidence and have low self-esteem. Solutions included: men should learn to trust their wives and women should behave well; women need to support each other more; adult literacy classes should be provided for women; girls should be educated to be future leaders; and men should assist more with the household chores. The successes, challenges and constraints of the programme are outlined and seven key recommendations made.

URL: http://www.fao.org/sd/Wpdirect/Wpre0130.htm

146   A state of two minds: state cultures, women, and politics in Kuwait
TÉTREAULT, MARY ANN. *International Journal of Middle East Studies* 33(2001)2, p. 203-220, lit.refs in notes ISSN 0020-7438
Kuwait, a small city-state on the Persian-Arabian Gulf, has undergone massive political, economic, and social development throughout the twentieth century. Despite this, Kuwaiti rulers still cherish what is perhaps an impossible dream: that Kuwait can be simultaneously a 'developed'

country and a 'traditional' tribally organized society run by an autocratic ruler. This dream is echoed in equally ambivalent pronouncements and policies regarding women, not only by representatives of the state but also by Kuwaiti citizens. Should Kuwaiti women stand side by side with men in public life, or should they be secluded, subjected by, and submissive to the men in their lives as local 'tradition' demands? These and other questions relating to the changing role, expectations and circumstances women in Kuwaiti society are addressed in the context of external pressures place on them by the family, the state, religion and modern life.

KIT Library code B 2454-33(2001)2

147   Political participation in the Pacific: issues of gender, race and religion
THOMAS, PAMELA. *Development Bulletin* (2002)59. Australian National University (ANU) Research School of Social Sciences. Developme. Studies Network, Canberra, 2002, 98 p. ill. lit.ref ISSN 1035-1132
This special issue focuses on the ways in which race, religion and gender individually and collectively influence politics and political participation in Pacific Island countries. It contains papers and discussions from a symposium 'Political participation in the Pacific issues of gender, race and religion', held in Australia, June 2002, and the output of a one-day workshop. The papers consider political participation from a variety of perspectives, including the personal stories of Pacific Island women and men who have been involved in local government, civil society and as political candidates in national elections. They concentrate on how issues of gender, race and religion impact on access to political participation. Underlying these themes there is consideration for the ways they may be linked t growing political instability and ethnic tension i the region. Together the papers highlight a widespread cultural prejudice against women's political involvement, women's political invisibility, the economic difficulties and often physical intimidation or violence women face in wanting to cast their own vote, let alone standin for election

KIT Library code E 3168-(2002)59

148   Women's movements and challenges t neopatrimonial rule: preliminary observations from Africa
TRIPP, AILI MARI. *Development and Change* 32(2001)1, p. 33-54, 41 lit.refs ISSN 0012-155X
Women's movements in Africa represent one of the key societal forces challenging state

lientelistic practices, the politicization of communal differences, and personalized rule. The 1980s and 1990s witnessed the demise of patronage-based women's wings that were tied to ruling parties, but also the concurrent growth of independent women's organizations with more far-reaching agendas. The emergence of such autonomous organizations has stemmed from the loss of state legitimacy, the opening up of political space, economic crisis, and the shrinking of state resources. Using examples from Africa, the paper shows why independent women's organizations and movements have often been well-situated to challenge clientelistic practices tied to the state. Gendered divisions of labour and organizational modes, coupled with the general exclusion of women from both formal and informal political arenas have defined women's relationship to the state, to power and to patronage. These characteristics have, on occasion, put women's movements in a position to challenge various state-linked patronage practices. Some of the implications of these challenges were explored here.

149   Lip-service and peanuts: the state and national machinery for women in Africa
TSIKATA, DZODZI. *National Machinery Series* 1. Third World Network-Africa (TWN-Africa), Accra, 2000, iv, 58 p. lit.refs ISSN 0855-4021 ISBN 9988-602-05-7
This NGO evaluation of the situation of national machinery for the advancement of women in Africa is based on the findings of the research in Botswana, Ghana, Morocco, Nigeria, Tanzania, Uganda, Zambia and Zimbabwe. It appeared that almost all of the national machinery suffered from a host of ills being placed in unsuitable locations, insufficient legal powers, too little political influence, and inadequate human and material resources. In some cases, these problems had been exacerbated by competition from other centres of power such as first ladies and their organizations, ruling parties' women's wings and influential NGO's. The absence of unequivocal commitment to gender equity on the part of governments, state institutions and civil society and its organizations and hostile economic environment created by neo-liberal paradigm in general and structural adjustment programmes (SAPs) in particular were also found to be a problem in most of the study countries. It was concluded that national machinery as presently constituted cannot deliver the Beijing Platform for Action, and that all the problems of national machinery had to be addressed in an integrated way. Governments in consultation with civil society organizations have to fundamentally rethink national machinery and ensure a proper demarcation of their functions, powers and their relationships with each other and with other players in order to avoid duplication of efforts and confusion among them. Governments have to become the primary financiers of national machinery instead of donors. In addition, they need to create an enabling environment for national machinery and be proactive in promoting gender equality policies.

150   Culture: the obstacle to active female participation in governance among the Igbo of Nigeria
UCHENDU, EGODI. *Asian Women* (2002)15, p. 73-93, 32 lit.refs ISSN 1225-925X
The Igbo is one of the three major sub nationalities in Nigeria, a country with about two hundred and fifty diverse ethnicities. Their political system can be described as democratic village republics. The people are generally patrilineal, attaching great importance to the masculine role and kinship ties. The submissive role of women in Igbo society, and Igbo men's controlling attitude toward them, were described. The political status of Igbo women is examined and the reasons why they have thus far been excluded from government analyzed. The structure of the pre-colonial Igbo society, especially the role and power of the Omu (female chiefs), is outlined. While illiteracy, poverty and the colonial experience are generally blamed for the poor participation of African women in politics, it is argued here that their absence from the political arena in Igboland is caused by Igbo culture itself which has systematically blocked their way from generation to generation. Igbo women are therefore urged to rally behind credible female political candidates to redress this gender imbalance.

151   Women's rights movements as a measure of African democracy
VAN ALLEN, JUDITH. In: A decade of democracy in Africa ed. by Stephen N. Ndegwa. *International Studies in Sociology and Social Anthropology* 81. Brill, Leiden, 2001, p. 39-63, 38 lit.refs ISSN 0074-8684
The currently dominant neoliberal narrative of democratization in Africa is silent on women, focusing on conflicts between male elites. Using the case of Botswana, this paper wants to present a counter-narrative of democratization that focuses on women's groups, along with trade unions, civic groups and other popular forces, as

annotated bibliography

a basis for 'democratization from below'. The inclusion of women in both politics and scholarly narratives is not only a question of equity. Examining conditions that make it possible for women's groups to organize and to succeed can provide a useful measure of the substantive democracy in a system, an understanding of the class base needed for effective mobilization of women and protection of their rights, and an idea of how women's groups might develop as part of effective coalitions seeking popular democracy. The mobilization and success of the women's rights movement in Botswana shows that democracy in Botswana is far from an empty formal claim. The Botswana case makes it clear how important it is for a women's movement to be autonomous, independent of political parties, and therefore able to generate its own agenda and priorities.
KIT Library code D 2025-(2001)81

152   The impact of democratic transitions on the representation of women in the national parliaments of Southern Africa
VAN KESSEL, INEKE. *African Century Publications Series* (2001)4, p. 116-130, ill. lit.refs in notes
Eastern Europe and sub-Saharan Africa make for an interesting comparison when looking at women's representation in parliament because of their simultaneous democratization processes, both of which occurred roundabout 1989. When the Soviet Union and countries of Eastern Europe adopted multi-party politics, the percentage of women in parliament dropped dramatically from an average of 30% to under 10%. This was partly due to the fact that the fixed quota system practised under communism was dropped, leaving women on the periphery of the political arena. Did the same thing happen to women in South Africa? In order to answer this question, the impact of democratization processes on participation by women, notably women's representation in parliament, was duly explored, focusing on developments within Eastern Europe and the Soviet Union, and parliaments in Southern Africa. Four points were examined: (1) women's representation in parliament under a one-party state; (2) women's representation after the democratic transition; (3) factors influencing the participation of women; and (4) whether political participation results in improvements in the quality of life for women and whether the quality of governance improves when women participate in politics. While no clear correlation between women's representation in parliament and the quality of life for women was found, research did show that women's presence is parliament is negatively correlated with corruption in government.
KIT Library code H 2783-(2001)4

153   A report on the politics of inclusion: Adivasi women in local governance in Karnataka
VIJAYALAKSHMI, V. *Gender, Technology and Development* 6(2002)2, p. 269-283, ill. 7 lit.refs
ISSN 0971-8524
It is often presumed that the problem of women participation is one of exclusion and that the solution lies in simply reserving fixed quotas of seats for women on local government bodies. No so. The issue is much more complex, as case studies of 40 Adivasi (tribal) women holding reserved seats on 'panchayats' in Mysore district Karnataka, India, illustrated. Adivasis are one o the most marginalized and disadvantaged social groups in India. Adivasi women have the added problem of gender inequity. Not surprisingly, their lack of control over areas of their own live low self esteem and strong feeling of alienation from the broader social and political structures generally made these women indifferent to their new political roles, while their low level of education, ignorance of government procedures and preoccupation with day-to-day survival mak them ineffective. As a result, Adivasi women's role in the traditional administration has been inconsequential. It was therefore concluded that the political empowerment of Adivasi women should be seen in conjunction with empowermen in other areas such as capability development and better access to information. So far, the non participation of Adivasi women in local governance is merely the continuation of the process of exclusion from other domains of life.
KIT Library code H 2516-6(2002)2

154   Liberal visions and actual power in grassroots civil society: local churches and women's empowerment in rural Malawi
VONDOEPP, PETER. *Journal of Modern African Studies* 40(2002)2,p. 273-301, ill. 43 lit.refs
ISSN 0022-278X
In 1996, a community study in rural Malawi examined the role of grass-roots Presbyterian and Catholic churches in empowering citizens, particularly women, in the political process. The local Catholic church was found to be more effective in fostering a nascent sense of political efficacy among women than the local Presbyterian churches, partly because it offered women an organizational environment wherein they could acquire important skills and take on unique public roles. What is notable about these findings is that the organizations that conformed most to the liberal ideal of civil society, the

Presbyterian churches, proved least effective in encouraging public engagement among marginalized citizens, while the highly 'illiberal' Catholic church was successful in this respect. To explain this finding, two issues were presented that expose problems in the liberal understanding of civil society, and underscore important themes in the ongoing debate. First, the study revealed that organizations with decentralized authority structures and internal democracy may fail to empower marginalized citizens, as they tend to reproduce and exacerbate local inequalities and conflicts within their structures. Second, corroborating critical views, the study highlighted the impact of power relations on the character and operation of civil society organizations. The adjusting power relations within organizations may be a prerequisite to their serving an empowering role with marginalized citizens.

KIT Library code A 1995-40(2002)2

155   Women's participation in local organizations: conditions and constraints
WEINBERGER, KATINKA; JUTTING, JOHANNES PAUL. *World Development* 29(2001)8, p. 1391-1404, 50 lit.refs
ISSN 0305-750X

Civic organizations have a capacity to contribute to economic growth and an equitable distribution of welfare by reducing information asymmetries and transaction costs. In an effort to contribute to the wider knowledge on the set-up of projects focused at increasing the organizational capacities of poor people, a pioneering study using a mixed methodological approach analyzed the determinants of participation in local development groups (LDGs) using data from two projects funded by UNDP in Kashmir and GTZ in Chad. One major finding was the 'middle-class effect' of participation. The exclusion by high majority of the poor was explained by high opportunity costs to join the group. It was also shown that an existing social network is a pre-condition for participation. In conclusion, further research should examine aspects such as the desirability of homogeneity in the groups; the type of activities/support being offered to groups; the relationship between participation and economic outcomes in different socio-economic settings; and the possibilities to lower transaction costs for individuals to join groups.

KIT Library code E 1271-29(2001)8

156   Women activists in Mali: the global discourse on human rights
WING, SUSANNA D. In: Women's activism and globalization: linking local struggles and transnational politics ed. by Nancy A. Naples & Manisha Desai. Routledge, New York, NY, 2002, p. 172-185, lit.refs in notes

Mali is one of the world's top 10 countries with the widest gap between men and women; more than 45% of Malian families are polygamous. At the same time, women constitute more than half of Mali's population and have a history of being politically active. They are also linked to one another by ethnicity and class, not just gender, and these links often transcend the urban/rural divide. It was argued here that the Malian government has created a space for female citizens to discuss their rights. The resulting dialogue on women's rights was linked to the participation of Malian women in a global discourse in which women leaders bridge the gap between the international community and local women. It was argued that in order to grasp the overall picture of human rights in Mali, understanding the interaction between women from urban and rural communities is critical. Following a brief discussion of women's interests and the relationship between globalization and women's rights, the strategies developed by women to strengthen their role in Mali's nascent democracy were analyzed. Interviews conducted in the regions of Koulikoro, Sikasso, Mopti, and Ségou in 1997-1998 offered insights into the role of women's associations in this process, especially organizations such as Association des Juristes Malienne (AJM), Groupe Féminin Droit de Suffrage (GFDS) and Observatoire des Droits de la Femme et de l'Enfant (ODEF). Finally, the critical role that associations and women play in nation building was analyzed.

KIT Library code P 02-1622

157   Constitutional dialogues: participation and citizenship in the transition towards democracy in Mali, 1991-1999
WING, SUSANNA DENHOLM. UMI, Ann Arbor, MI, 2002, xviii, 279 p. ill. bibliogr.: p. 252-279
Doctoral diss. University of California, Los Angeles, 2000.

This book about participation and citizenship in Mali includes a chapter on ways in which women are promoting their participation in the country's nascent democracy. In particular the role played by women's associations in the democratization process is analyzed using data from interviews conducted in the regions of Koulikoro, Sikasso, Mopti and Ségou in 1994 and 1997-1998. The analysis focuses on associations such as the Association des Juristes Maliennes (an association of female lawyers), Groupe Féminin Droit de Suffrage (a group for women's voting rights) and Observatoire des Droits de la Femme et de l'Enfant (a watch group for the protection of the rights of women and children). It is found that despite their diverse backgrounds, women have similar interests as women and therefore many have chosen to organize themselves in gender-based associations. One of the reasons many women are prevented from exercizing their rights is that they do not know of the existence of such rights. This is complicated by low female literacy and low gender and legal awareness, which are a result, in part, of gender relations. These barriers to dialogue must be overcome in order for women to participate effectively in constitutional dialogues. The examples presented explain the ways in which associations are addressing this issue.

KIT Library code P 01-3025

158   Women and political empowerment manual
UNIFEM Pacific, Suva, 1999
During the 1995 Fourth World Conference on Women and the World NGO Forum in Beijing the need for political empowerment of women was highlighted, with the UN and individual governments setting a target to increase the number of women participants in local and national decision making to half the total. This manual will help Pacific nations meet this target. It enables women to prepare mentally and managerially for the move into political life. It is meant for prospective politicians and for any woman interested in the political process, voters, those wanting to join political parties, members of campaign teams and women's interest groups. The manual comprises the following sections: (1) why women need to enter politics in the Pacific and the barriers they face; (2) the concept of good governance; (3) the different forms of government and electoral systems in the Pacific; (4) the personal attributes and support systems required by women to be successful politicians; (5) how to run the campaign team and candidate through the campaign; and (6) how parliamentary life looks like for the elected politician and how to cope with the job and the personal pressures that a newly elected politician faces.

URL: http://www.unifempacific.com/resources/
publications/pol-empower/

159   Women in government: 50/50 by 2005. Get the balance right! Asia Pacific Workshop on gender balance in political representation, 21-22 March 2001
The workshop took place in Manila, Philippines from 21 to 22 March 2001 and attracted 60 participants from 10 countries from South and Southeast Asia. Its theme was '50/50 by 2005: Get the Balance Right'. An integrative summary of workshop sessions was presented along with a number of strategies and issues that were raised during the two-day workshop. The following concerns were addressed: (1) what is gender balance and why it is needed; (2) how women's participation in politics as citizens, candidates and legislators can transform politics; and (3) a range of strategies to attain gender balance. Sub-regional action plans to attain gender balance were also included, focusing on affirmative strategies such as: quotas; gender mainstreaming; gender sensitization of men; leadership and candidate training; legislative support services for elected women; constituency linkaging; information development and dissemination; networking and alliance building; and public awareness raising. Finally, the contribution of donor agencies to this process was outlined, focusing on areas such as women's human rights, citizen participation, political leadership, governance and gender budget analysis.

URL: http://www.cld.org/ManilaConference.htm

160   Women and leadership: voices for security and development. Forum report
South Asia Partnership, Ottawa, 2002
In November 2002, the South Asia Partnership (SAP) in Canada, hosted a two-day forum in Ottawa to explore the issue of insecurity, especially concerning women in developing countries where arms have become a community development issue and represent a serious threat to peace-building and prosperity in South Asian communities. Presentations highlighted the current situation in a number of Asian countries and regions, including Nepal, Afghanistan, Assam, Nagaland and Manipur, India, Pakistan, Bangladesh, and Sri Lanka. The activities, goals and achievements of local grass-roots women's movements, including the daily challenges their members face at the hands of male-dominated governments and institutions, ranging from intimidation and harassment to outright assassination attempts, were reported. Other contributions to the debate came from the Canadian Committee for the United Nations Development Fund for Women (UNIFEM), the United Nations High Commission for Refugees (UNHCR), the International Development Research Centre (IDRC), and the Canadian Department of Foreign Affairs and International Trade (DFAIT).

URL: http://action.web.ca/home/sap/attach/
Gender%20ReportFinal.pdf

**161	Women, nationality and citizenship**
Women 2000 and Beyond, June 2003. Division for
the Advancement of Women (DAW). United
Nations (UN), New York, NY, 2003
This issue of 'Women 2000 and Beyond' discusses
discrimination against women in nationality laws.
It examines laws that differentiate between
women and men in the acquisition and retention of
nationality, as well as in relation to the nationality
of their children, highlighting the legal and
practical disadvantages such laws cause. It shows
how international law is used to address
discrimination in nationality laws and surveys
national and international case law on
discrimination in nationality laws, taking into
consideration how human rights norms relating to
freedom of movement, freedom of information,
family rights and other rights have been
increasingly applied. Approaches adopted by
states to avoid gender-based discrimination are
analyzed and measures are recommended for
states and NGOs to ensure compliance with human
rights standards in the context of nationality.
URL: http://www.un.org/womenwatch/daw/public/
index.html#w2-jun03

**162	Women's political participation and
good governance: 21st century challenges**
United Nations Development Programme
(UNDP), New York, NY, 2000
Drawing on a UNDP-sponsored meeting on
Women's Political Participation-21st Century
Challenges in 1999, this publication focuses on
issues including progress made in women's
political participation since Beijing (Fourth
World Conference of Women, 1995), the Indian
experiment with constitutional amendments
mandating the reservation of one-third of local
government-elected representation to women, and
the wider connection between gender, poverty and
governance. It also highlights the South African
Women's Budget, Uganda's experience with new
political alliances for gender and politics, and
explores the policy responses to gender-based
violence. One central theme is that the continued
absence of women's voices in governance is
largely due to inequitable representation and
participation in institutional structures, from
governments and political parties to NGOs and
the private sector. However, it also recognizes
that boosting women's political participation
needs to go beyond raw numbers to encompass
the complex relationship between power, poverty
and participation. Women want and need to be able
to participate in the decisions that affect them,
their families, communities and countries.
URL: http://magnet.undp.org/new/pdf/gender/wpp/
women_book.pdf

**163	Gender & nation**
YUVAL-DAVIS, NIRA. *Politics and culture: a
theory, culture & society series*. Sage, London,
2000, x, 157 p. bibliogr.: p. 135-148
ISBN 0-8039-8664-5
Gender relations affect and are affected by
national projects and processes. The
intersections between gender and nation are
examined moving from the role of women as
biological reproducers of the nation, through
their roles in the cultural constructions of
nations, to the ways civil constructions of
nationhood, via rights and duties of citizenship,
are gendered. The chapters focus on: (1) women's
roles as symbolic border guards and as
embodiments of the collectivity, while at the
same time being its cultural reproducers is
looked at, taking into account issues of religion
and culture, and globalization; (2) the effects of
gender relations, but also of factors such as
ethnicity, class, place on constructions of
citizenship and distributions of citizenship rights;
and (3) constructions of manhood and
womanhood, which have been linked to
participation in militaries and in wars, and how
those have been linked to citizenship rights and
other social divisions such as ethnicity and class.
The relationship between womanhood, feminism
and peace is also discussed. Finally, questions of
gender, nations and the politics of women's
empowerment are addressed by examining
women's cooperation with and resistance to
nationalist struggles on the one hand and
international feminist politics on the other.
KIT Library code N 01-272

**164	Islam and the politics of community
and citizenship**
ZUBAIDA, SAMI. *Middle East Report* (2001)221,
p. 20-27, ill. lit.refs in notes ISSN 0899-2851
Political Islam in itself is no longer the major
issue in Middle East politics. Democratization
and welfare are. In this context, the role, impact
and challenges facing civil society in several
different Middle Eastern countries are explored.
It is argued that Islamists' credibility as political
alternatives hinges upon the alternatives they
can present to authoritarian government and the
skewed distribution of wealth and resources. As
the current crisis exacerbated by 9/11 and the
war in Iraq, reinforces the regimes' propensity to
place security above all other concerns, political
Islam faces a heightened challenge. Radical and
violent Islamic movements in most Middle
Eastern countries are now on the retreat: they
have been almost totally neutralized in Egypt, are
the targets of massive state repression in
Algeria, and Hizballah in Lebanon has become

domesticated into a national political party.
Radical Islamists' rhetoric is maintained only in
exile. Yet, it is also pointed out that the modern
Arab state combines the ruler/subject model of
the dynastic state and the totalitarian model of a
degenerate Leninist state. Besides Israel, only
Turkey and Iran in the Middle East have the kind
of electoral politics which can lead to changes of
governments. Issues such as: human rights;
democracy; anti-Western feeling; survival as
resistance; conservatives and radicals; and
making space for citizens are discussed in this
context. It is concluded that it would be foolish to
try to predict the long-term consequences of the
present crisis: we can only note the trends.
KIT Library code H 1879-(2001)221

gender, citizenship and governance

Author index

(numbers refer to abstract numbers)

Abdela, Lesley, 001
Afshar, Haleh, 002
Ahern, Patricia, 003
Akiiki, Kuruhiira G.M.A., 004
Al-Hamad, Laila, 005
Amadiume, Ifi, 006
Anderson, Shelley, 007
Angeles, Leonora C., 008
Atienza, Maria Ela L., 010
Aubrey, Lisa, 011

Baksh-Sodeen, Rawwida, 012
Baldez, Lisa, 013
Banerjee, Sikata, 014
Bell, Emma, 015, 016
Bertinussen, Gudrun, 076
Bessell, Sharon, 017
Bhattachan, Krishna Bahadur, 087
Bouta, T., 018
Boyd, Rosalind, 019
Bradshaw, Sarah, 020
Brookfield, Christine, 021
Brown, Andrea M., 022
Budlender, Debbie, 023, 024, 025
Butegwa, Florence, 026
Bystydzienski, Jill M., 027

Cagan, Elizabeth, 028
Çagatay, Nilufer, 029
Campbell, Horace, 030
Chin, Mikyung, 031
Choudhury, Dilara, 032
Clark, Cal, 080
Clark, Fiona C., 100, 101
Clulow, Michael, 033
Cornwall, Andrea, 034

Dauda, Carol L., 035
Dollar, David, 036
Douglas, Bronwen, 037
Dupree, Lila, 038

Emadi, Hafizullah, 039
Esim, Simel, 041
Espine-Villaluz, Sheila, 042
Etchart, Linda, 012

Fisman, Raymond, 036
Fitzsimmons, Tracy, 044
Fonjong, Lotsmart, 045
Franceschet, Susan, 111
Frerks, G., 018
Friedman, Elisabeth J., 046

Gatti, Roberta, 036
Ghosh, Bhola Nath, 052
Goetz, Anne Marie, 053, 054, 055, 056
Gramberger, Marc, 057
Gray, Tricia Jean, 058, 059

Hansen, G., 060
Haque, M. Shamsul, 061
Hassim, Shireen, 055, 056
Hewitt, Guy, 025
Hickey, Sam, 062
Hofbauer Balmori, Helena, 063
Höglund, Anna T., 064
Holvoet, Nathalie, 065
Htun, Mala N., 066
Huffer, Elise, 067
Huq, Shireen P., 068

Jacobs, Susie, 069
Jacobson, Ruth, 069
Jaeckel, Monika, 070
Jenkins, Rob, 053
Johnson Sirleaf, Ellen, 128
Jones, Mark P., 066
Joseph, Neena, 47
Joseph, Suad, 072
Jutting, Johannes Paul, 155

Kabeer, Naila, 074
Kandil, Amani, 075
Kandiyoti, Deniz, 072
Karamé, Kari H., 076
Kelleher, David, 125
Kinuthia-Njenga, Cecilia, 077
Kumar Mohapatra, Ajaya, 078

Lee, Eliza W.Y., 079
Lee, Rose J., 080
Lee, Sunju, 081
Leslie, Helen, 082
Longwe, Sara Hlupekile, 083
Lundkvist, Helen, 084

Mama, Amina, 086
Manandhar, Laxmi Keshari, 087
Marchbank, Jen, 069
Masterson, Julia M., 003
Mazurana, Dyan, 089
McFadden, Patricia, 088
McKay, Susan, 089
Meintjes, Sheila, 090
Menon-Sen, Kalyani, 091
Merrifield, Juliet, 092
Mir-Hosseini, Ziba, 093
Mitchell, Suzette, 094
Moghadam, Valentine M., 095
Mojab, Shahrzad, 096
Molisa, Grace Mera, 067

Molyneux, Maxine, 097
Morna, C.L., 099
Moser, Caroline O.N., 100, 101
Mugisha, Maude, 102
Muigai, Wanjiru, 103
Mukhopadhyay, Maitrayee, 104
Myers, Roxanne, 105

Naraghi-Anderlini, Sanam B., 106
Nath, Vikas, 107
Nuti, Paul, 003
Nyamu, Celestine Itumbi, 108

Ofei-Aboagye, Esther, 109
Ogunsanya, Kemi, 038
Ohene-Konadu, Gifty, 110
Okeke-Ihejirika, Philomina E., 111
Okome Mojubaolu, Olufunke, 112, 113
Onsarigo, Beatrice, 114
Osirim, Mary Johnson, 115
Osman, Amira, 116

Palier, Judith Ann, 117
Parpart, Jane L., 119
Patterson, Amy, 120
Piza-Lopez, Eugenia, 121
Purusi Sadiki, Jean-Jacques, 123

Rai, Shirin M., 124
Rao, Aruna, 125
Razavi, Shahra, 097, 126
Reeves, Hazel, 127
Rehn, Elisabeth, 128
Reyes, Melanie M., 042
Riordan, Siobhan, 129
Rizzo, Helen Mary, 130

Saito, Fumihiko, 131
Sarraf, Feridoun, 132
Schild, Verónica, 133
Seeta Prabhu, K., 091
Sekhon, Joti, 027
Sever, Charlie, 127
Sharma, Kumud, 134
Singh, Raj, 135
Sinha, Niroj, 136
Skjelsbaek, Inger, 137
Smith, Dan, 137
Stevenson, Linda S., 138
Sweetman, Caroline, 140

Tamale, Sylvia, 141, 142, 143
Tempelman, D.E., 145
Tétreault, Mary Ann, 146
Thomas, Pamela, 147
Tripp, Aili Mari, 148
Tryggestad, Torunn L., 076
Tsikata, Dzodzi, 149

Uchendu, Egodi, 150

Van Allen, Judith, 151
Van Kessel, Ineke, 152
Vijayalakshmi, V., 153
VonDoepp, Peter, 154

Weinberger, Katinka, 155
Wing, Susanna D., 156, 157

Yuval-Davis, Nira, 163

Zubaida, Sami, 164

gender, citizenship and governance

Geographical index

(numbers refer to abstract numbers)

Afghanistan, 002, 039, 160
Africa, 006, 011, 019, 026, 038, 076, 083, 088, 089,
090, 101, 114, 118, 123, 142, 148, 149
Algeria, 072
Angola, 030, 090
Arab Countries, 005, 095, 124
Argentina, 058
Asia, 009, 089
Australia, 021, 025, 027, 124

Bangladesh, 032, 068, 104, 107, 140, 144, 160
Belgium, 027
Belize, 016
Botswana, 084, 124, 140, 151
Brazil, 048, 069
Burundi, 019, 090

Cameroon, 016, 045, 062
Canada, 021, 027, 084
Caribbean Region, 105
Central Africa, 123
Chad, 155
Chile, 013, 016, 044, 058, 059, 097, 111, 133
China, 069, 080
Colombia, 100, 101, 137
Congo, 019
Croatia, 101

Dominican Republic, 060

East Asia, 080
Eastern Europe, 124, 152
Ecuador, 021, 084
Egypt, 005, 027, 072, 075
El Salvador, 027, 028, 033, 101
Eritrea, 027
Ethiopia, 016
Europe, 137

Fiji, 017

Ghana, 011, 021, 109, 110
Guatemala, 021, 101, 124, 140
Guinea, 016
Guyana, 105, 107

Honduras, 027
Hong Kong, 027, 079

India, 014, 027, 052, 053, 069, 073, 078, 091, 097,
101, 104, 107, 124, 134, 135, 136, 153, 160
Iran, 072, 093, 096, 097
Iraq, 072, 096

Ireland, 027, 069
Israel, 072, 076, 101

Jamaica, 016
Japan, 080
Jordan, 072

Kenya, 011, 077, 103, 108
Kosova, 002
Kuwait, 130, 146

Latin America, 025, 028, 044, 066, 089, 100, 137
Lebanon, 072, 076

Malawi, 154
Malaysia, 097
Mali, 156, 157
Melanesia, 037
Mexico, 025, 097, 117, 124, 138
Middle East, 064, 072, 096, 164
Morocco, 072

Namibia, 016, 104
Nepal, 087, 144, 160
Nicaragua, 020
Nigeria, 006, 086, 111, 112, 113, 150

Oceania, 009, 089, 147, 158

Pakistan, 104, 124, 144, 160
Palestine, 002, 072, 101
Papua New Guinea, 016, 017
Peru, 097
Philippines, 008, 010, 016, 021, 025, 051, 080
Poland, 027, 060, 097

Russia, 027
Rwanda, 019, 025

Saudi Arabia, 072
Senegal, 120
Serbia, 064
Sierra Leone, 012
Singapore, 027, 061
Somalia, 064
South Africa, 006, 021, 025, 027, 051, 055, 056, 060,
069, 090, 097, 098, 104, 124
South Asia, 049, 104, 137, 159
South East Asia, 159
South Korea, 021, 025, 031, 080, 081, 089
Southern Africa, 049, 064, 099, 104, 152
Sri Lanka, 104, 137, 160
Sudan, 072, 090, 116
Sweden, 021, 051, 084
Syria, 027

Taiwan, 080
Tanzania, 022, 048, 139

Tonga, 016
Trinidad and Tobago, 051
Tunisia, 072
Turkey, 021, 072, 096

Uganda, 004, 016, 019, 035, 054, 055, 056, 097, 102,
131, 140, 141, 143, 145
Ukraine, 107
United Kingdom, 006, 025, 101, 124, 129
United States, 027, 076

Vanuatu, 067
Venezuela, 046
Vietnam, 008, 094

Yemen, 072
Yugoslavia, 137

Zambia, 016, 104
Zimbabwe, 035, 104, 115

gender, citizenship and governance

Web resources

Asia Pacific Forum on Women, Law and Development (APWLD)
http://www.apwld.org
APWLD is an NGO committed to enabling women to use law as an instrument of social change for equality, justice and development. The site contains information on the APWLD programmes, including 'Women's participation in political process', and 'Feminist legal theory & practice training'. Other sections present publications, forum news, statements and links.

Centre for Asia Pacific Women in Politics (CAPWIP)
http://www.capwip.org
CAPWIP is a regional NGO dedicated to promoting equal participation of women in politics and decision making. It operates through a network of national affiliates clustered into 5 sub-regional groups: Central Asia, East Asia, Pacific, South East Asia and South Asia. The website contains information on the activities, measures of women's political participation, and information resources.

Commonwealth Gender Management System Publications
http://www.thecommonwealth.org/gender/htm/pu blications/gender_manage_pdfs.htm
This series of guides and manuals on gender mainstreaming for governments and other stakeholders includes background papers and other material on the Gender Budget initiative, and guidelines to do a gender-sensitive budget analysis.

Democracy through partnership between men and women, Inter-Parliamentary Union (IPU)
http://www.ipu.org/iss-e/women.htm
The IPU has studied a series of issues of direct concern to women. This website offers information on what the IPU is doing in the field of women and gender, provides access to a database on 'women in politics', and reports statistical data on women in national parliaments by country, and also world and regional averages.
Empowerment, World Bank
http://1nweb18.org/ESSD/sdvext.nsf/68ParentDoc/ Empowerment?Opendocument
This site on empowerment presents information on projects being designed in Ethiopia and India, ongoing work on measuring empowerment, and work on empowerment and poverty reduction strategies. A section with resources on empowerment, a newsletter and links to upcoming empowerment-related events are also offered.

Gender and governance resources, the Centre for Legislative Development (CLD)
http://www.cld.org
The site offers access to various publications and information on gender and governance and in particular on the national campaign for 50-50 in government.

Gender and local governance, Netherlands Development Organization (SNV)
http://www.kit.nl/assets/images/Gender_and_local _Governance.doc
Information package including a handbook containing various strategies and best practices on how to engender governance at a local level, with special reference to West Africa. It also includes lists of websites, e-mail lists, and toolkits. Published in April 2001.

Gender and peacekeeping online training course
http://www.genderandpeacekeeping.org
Participant and instructor training modules are offered in addition to relevant references, resources and links.

Gender and political participation, International Institute for Democracy and Electoral Assistance (IDEA)
http://www.idea.int/gender/index.htm
As part of the Gender and Political Participation project, this website presents information on IDEA's work and other activities in this field, and

provides access to the Global Database of Quotas for Women.

Gender, Citizenship and Governance programme, Royal Tropical Institute (KIT)
http://www.kit.nl/gcg/
The website of KIT's GCG programme which focuses on innovative gender and governance initiatives in South Asia and South Africa, provides information about the programme, the projects and other work undertaken, and provides links to relevant resources.

Gender, decentralization and public finance, World Bank
http://www.worldbank.org/wbi/publicfinance/decentralization/gender.htm
The site presents links to websites, articles and events in the field of gender and decentralization & public finance, including on the issues of gender responsive budgeting, local governance, and poverty.

Gender in parliament, Women'sNet
http://womensnet.org.za/parliament/parliament
This information resource is about women's equality work that is taking place in national, provincial and local governments and legislatures in South Africa.

Gender-Responsive Budget Initiative (GRBI)
http://www.gender-budgets.org
The Initiative is a collaborative effort of the United Nations Development Fund for Women (UNIFEM), the Commonwealth Secretariat, and the International Development Research Centre (IDRC) to support government and civil society in analyzing national and local budgets from a gender perspective and applying this analysis to the formulation of gender responsive budgets. The website discusses events and activities, provides access to a document library, and gives information on GRBI projects, activities, events, and links.

Governance, Gender & Development, Asian Development Bank (ADB)
http://www.adb.org/gender/practices/governance/default.asp
The Governance section provides access to information on gender and governance issues in Nepal, Pakistan and Bangladesh, as well as about regional technical assistance on the issue.

Governance, peace and security programme, United Nations Development Fund for Women (UNIFEM), Arab States Regional Office
http://www.unifem.org.jo/governance

Governance Resource Centre (GRC) Exchange
http://www.grc-exchange.org
Hosted by the Governance Resource Centre of the UK Department for International Development, the website aims to share the latest information about governance in development. The site presents lists of key texts and resources by theme; summaries of documents, links to documents and organizations, and information on training opportunities and events.

Information Gateway on women in local government, International Union of Local Authorities (IULA)
http://www.iula-int.org/iula/left.asp?L=EN&ID=164&old=17
The Information Gateway provides access to reports, articles, case studies and other documents.

International Women's Democracy Centre (IWDC)
http://www.iwdc.org/
IWDC is a non-profit organization offering training aimed at increasing women's political participation. Training programmes for women focus on running for elected office, campaign management, advocacy, fundraising and using communications technology.

Online women in politics.org, Asia Pacific Online Network of Women in Governance, Politics, and Transformative Leadership
http://www.onlinewomeninpolitics.org
In various sections, information is provided on regional and country features, events, statistics, women's situation, and campaigns. The site also provides access (after registration) to the online training module 'Making Governance Gender-Responsive.'

PeaceWomen, Women's International League for Peace and Freedom (WILPF)
http://www.peacewomen.org
The website works towards rapid and full implementation of UN Security Council Resolution 1325 on Women, Peace and Security. To this end, PeaceWomen seeks to provide a clearinghouse for accurate and timely information on the impact of armed conflict on women, and women's peace building efforts to facilitate communication among women peace activists and between women activists and the UN system. The website provides information on the adoption of the Security Council Resolution 1325 on women, the UN, resources, and organizations.

Toolkit Citizen Participation
http://www.toolkitparticipation.com
This toolkit offers information on tools that
promote citizen participation in local governance.
Over 100 cases are described and analysed. The
site also presents articles and links for further
reference.

Women building peace: from the village council
to the negotiating table
**http://www.international-alert.org/women/
new2.html**
Women building peace is an international
campaign launched by International Alert to
place women, peace and security on the
international agenda. The website offers an
overview of the campaign, its publications, and
activities.

Women in Local Development, Human
Settlements, United Nations Economic and Social
Commission for Asia and the Pacific (UNESCAP)
http://www.unescap.org/huset/women
This site provides links to country reports and
other documents on the state of women in urban
local government.

Women in Local Government, Regional
Information Resource Facility (RIRF-WLG)
http://www.decentralization.ws/rirf/index.htm
An online resource that houses a compendium of
research output, conference papers, gender
statistics, and articles on women in local
governance across Asia and the Pacific.

Women in Security, Conflict Management and
Peace (WISCOMP), Foundation for Universal
Responsibility of His Holiness the Dalai Lama,
New Delhi, India
http://www.furhhdl.org/wiscompindex.htm
Planned as a South Asian initiative, WISCOMP
promotes the national, regional and global
leadership of women by enhancing their
participation and expertise in the areas of
security, non-violent engagement, conflict
transformation and multi-track diplomacy.

Women of the World, WomenWatch, United
Nations (UN)
http://www.un.org/womenwatch/world/
Maintained by WomenWatch, this list of country
profiles provides information on national reports
to the Committee on the Elimination of
Discrimination Against Women (CEDAW) and to
the Fourth World Conference on Women (FWCW).

Women's Learning Partnership for Rights,
Development, and Peace (WLP)
http://www.learningpartnership.org
WLP is an international NGO that aims to
empower women and girls through leadership
training, supporting capacity building, and
helping women generate and receive information
and knowledge. The website provides access to
legislation on women's conventions, and includes
bibliographies by subject, including women and
leadership, and by region, facts and figures, and
audio and video excerpts reflecting women's
voices.

Women's political participation, Centre for
Development and Population Activities (CEDPA)
**http://www.cedpa.org/keyissues/womenspolitical.
html**
CEDPA is a network of organizations that aims at
empowering women. Women's political
participation and leadership training are among
the key issues of CEDPA's work. Information
about their projects, training and publications in
these as well as other fields of work is presented
at the website.

WomenWatch
http://www.un.org/womenwatch
WomenWatch is the gateway on the advancement
and empowerment of women. It provides access
to information and resources on the promotion of
gender equality throughout the UN system,
including the UN Secretariat, regional
commissions, funds, programmes, and
specialized agencies.

About the authors

Cathi Albertyn founded the Gender Research Project at the Centre for Applied Legal Studies (CALS), University of the Witwatersrand, in 1992 and became involved in advocating for gender equality and women's rights in the new South African Constitution. She has managed and engaged in a variety of research projects that sought to inform the development of new policies and laws in South Africa after the achievement of democracy in 1994. She has researched and written extensively in the areas of gender, law and human rights, especially on equality, reproductive rights, HIV/AIDS and the place of women in the transition to democracy. Cathi is currently the Director of the Centre for Applied Legal Studies and is working on a research project that evaluates progress towards gender equality by the South African government.
Contact address:
Centre for Applied Legal Studies (CALS), University of the Witwatersrand,
Private Bag 3, Wits 2050, South Africa
Tel: +27 11 717-8600
Fax: +27 11 403-2341
Email: albertync@law.wits.ac.za
Website: www.law.wits.ac.za/cals/

Liz Frank grew up in Germany and Australia and was a teacher in both countries. She moved to Namibia in 1990 to support the post-independence reform in education. A year later she joined Sister Namibia, first as a volunteer and currently as director, and she is the editor of the Sister Namibia magazine. She has conducted research on women's participation in politics and decision making and on the socio-cultural discourse relating to women's reproductive and sexual health and rights in Namibia.
Contact address:
Sister Namibia
P.O. Box 40092, Windhoek, Namibia
Tel: +264 61 230618/230757
Fax: +264 61 236371
E-mail: sister@iafrica.com.na

Elizabeth Khaxas is a feminist, a community activist, educator and a lesbian who grew up in Namibia. She is a founding member of Sister Namibia and Women's Solidarity, two feminist organizations, and of the Rainbow Project, an organization promoting the equal human rights of gay and lesbian people in Namibia. She has worked extensively on issues of violence against women, women's participation in politics and decision making, and on human rights for gay and lesbian people.

about the authors

133

Elizabeth is currently a consultant for Sister Namibia.

Contact address:
Sister Namibia
P.O. Box 40092, Windhoek, Namibia
Tel: +264 61 230618/230757
Fax: +264 61 236371
E-mail: sister@iafrica.com.na

Likhapha Mbatha is a researcher and Acting Head of the Gender Research Project at the Centre for Applied Legal Studies (CALS), University of the Witwatersrand. The focus of her work is on customary law issues. She is a member of the Project Committee of the South African Law Reform Commission working on the reform of customary law and has been engaged in action-oriented research to monitor the implementation of the Recognition of Customary Marriages Act. Her recent publications include the article 'Reforming the customary law of succession' in the South African Journal of Human Rights, vol. 18, part 2 (2002), p. 259-286, and a chapter in 'Democratising local government: problems and opportunities in the advancement of gender equality' (Zed, 2003). Likhapha has been involved in KIT's Gender Citizenship Governance programme and is co-author (with Cathi Albertyn) of a South African case study 'Law reform process around the customary law in South Africa' in the KIT Research Report 'Creating voice, carving space: defending good governance from a gender Perspective' (July 2003).

Contact address:
Centre for Applied Legal Studies (CALS), University of the Witwatersrand
Private Bag 3, Wits 2050, South Africa
Tel: +27 11 717-8600
Fax: +27 11 403-2341
E-mail: mbathal@law.wits.ac.za
Website: www.law.wits.ac.za/cals/

Naeem Mirza
Contact address:
Aurat Foundation
Hs. No. 16, St. 67, G-6/4, Islamabad, Pakistan
Tel: +92 51 2277512/2277547
Fax: +92 51 2822060
E-mail: Apisf@isb.sdnpk.org; Naeemamirza@yahoo.com

Maitrayee Mukhopadhyay is the Area Leader for Social Development and Gender Equity in the Department of Development Policy and Practice at the Royal Tropical Institute, Amsterdam. She received her PhD in Social Anthropology at the University of Sussex. Her thesis research focused on women's experiences of litigation under the personal laws (those that cover marriage and inheritance) in India. The study raised vital questions regarding identity and citizenship in Indian democracy. Maitrayee has worked on rural and urban development policy and programming in Asia and Africa for the last twenty years and her special area of interest and expertise is gender issues in development. In her current position she is involved in developing and teaching international courses on gender and development, providing technical support to development agencies and undertaking research. In the last four years she has developed a special focus on citizenship and participatory governance and its relevance to development policy and practice and has led an inter-regional action research programme on Gender, Citizenship and Governance. Maitrayee has published extensively on gender and development issues. Her most recent publication Governing for Equity' analyzes the findings of the Gender, Citizenship and Governance action research programme.

Contact address:
Social Development & Gender Equity Area
KIT Development, Policy and Practice, Royal Tropical Institute (KIT),
P.O. Box 95001, 1090 HA, Amsterdam, the Netherlands
Tel: +31 20-568 8271
E-mail: m.mukhopadhyay@kit.nl
Website: www.kit.nl/development/

Aleyamma Vijayan is coordinator of Sakhi, a resource centre for women in Kerala, India, which she initiated in 1996. Having gained her Masters in Social Work, she has spent 17 years of work in the field of fishing communities at various levels and in various capacities, including as country coordinator of the 'Women in Fisheries' programme. She has been one of the initiators of the Self Employed Women's Association (SEWA) and has helped bring together autonous women's groups in Kerala under a common banner called Kerala streevedi, the only non-party based women's movement in Kerala taking up issues of women in the state.

Contact address:
Sakhi Women's Resource Centre
Convent Road, Trivandrum-695035, Kerala, India
Tel: +91 471 2462251

Minke Valk, **Sarah Cummings** and **Henk van Dam** are information specialists within the Information and Library Services Department of KIT (Royal Tropical Institute) in the Netherlands. They are editors of the Gender, Society & Development series.

Contact address:
Information and Library Services (ILS), KIT (Royal Tropical Institute)
P.O. Box 95001, 1090 HA Amsterdam, the Netherlands
Tel: +31 20-568 8344 / 8594/ 8573/
E-mail: m.valk@kit.nl; s.cummings@kit.nl; h.v.dam@kit.nl
Website: http://www.kit.nl/ils/
Website: http://www.kit.nl/ils/html/gender_society_development.asp
Website: http://www.kit.nl/specials/

about the authors

135

QM LIBRARY
(MILE END)